To Ruth 10-19-02

Ed Ulrich

Out There Beyond Beyond

Elaine Ulrich

Ed Ulrich has learned
"Out There Beyond Be
required text in two class
Messiah College. One cou
written course about autobio es,
and memories. The other is a freshman
class at Washington Bible College, as
a written research project.

Out There Beyond *Beyond*

The Story of Ed and Elaine Ulrich

Edward W. Ulrich

with Larry M. Lake

CHRISTIAN PUBLICATIONS, INC.
CAMP HILL, PENNSYLVANIA

Christian Publications, Inc.
3825 Hartzdale Drive, Camp Hill, PA 17011
www.cpi-horizon.com
www.christianpublications.com

Faithful, biblical publishing since 1883

Out There Beyond Beyond
ISBN: 0-87509-881-9
LOC Catalog Card Number: 99-080100

Printed in the United States of America

00 01 02 03 04 5 4 3 2 1

Cover portrait by Karl Foster

Additional photos provided by Myron Bromley, Gordon Larson and Dick Lenehan

Out in the chartless Guinea hills
the pigment is in reverse;
black is the mark of the royal line
and clothing a useless curse;
and the drums give tone to their hopes and fears
as you lower your wing where the jungle clears
to meet the naked men with spears
who come to the native bourse.

You have no creed or code or law
to share with the Stone Age clan;
and all you know is that they, like you,
are made in the mold of man;
so you arm your face with a friendly smile
and you open your hand to deny your guile,
and the ages shrink for a little while
out there beyond beyond.

The poem, by the former airline pilot who was then the editor of *Flying,* was published with Ed Ulrich's article, "Pilot Beyond Beyond," in the August 1958 issue.

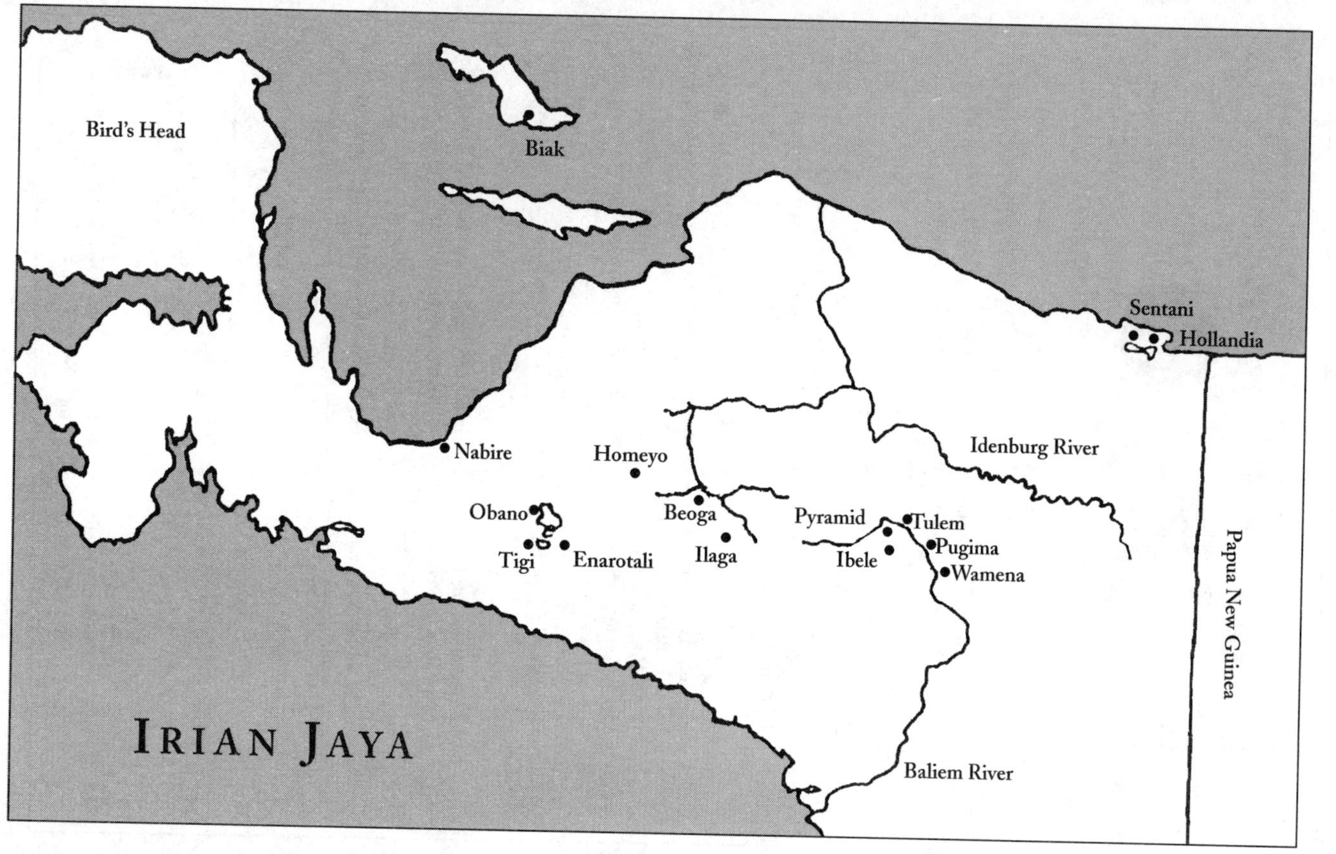
Bird's Head
Biak
Sentani
Hollandia
Nabire
Homeyo
Idenburg River
Obano
Beoga
Pyramid
Tulem
Pugima
Wamena
Tigi
Enarotali
Ilaga
Ibele
Papua New Guinea
IRIAN JAYA
Baliem River

OFFICERS

REV. H. M. SHUMAN
PRESIDENT

REV. WILLIAM CHRISTIE
VICE PRESIDENT
TREASURER

REV. E. J. RICHARDS
GENERAL SECRETARY

REV. S. W. MCGARVEY
HOME SECRETARY

REV. DAVID J. FANT
PUBLICATION SECRETARY

REV. A. C. SNEAD
FOREIGN SECRETARY

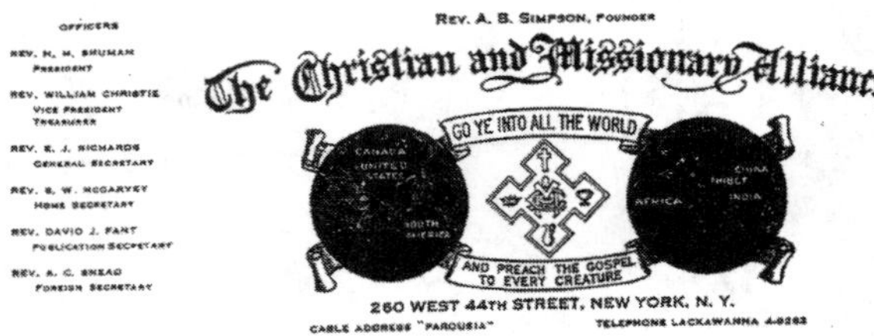

FOREIGN MISSION FIELDS

INDIA
FRENCH WEST AFRICA
CONGO
GABON
FRENCH INDO-CHINA & SIAM
COLOMBIA
ECUADOR
PERU
CHILE
ARGENTINA
KANSU-TIBETAN BORDER
KWEICHOW-SZECHUAN
CENTRAL CHINA & SHANGHAI
SOUTH CHINA
PALESTINE-ARABIAN BORDER
JAPAN
PHILIPPINE ISLANDS
NETHERLANDS EAST INDIES
PUERTO RICO
JAMAICA

March 1, 1939

Record of Conversation between Mr. and Mrs. William G. Jaffray and A.C. Snead concerning purchase of airplane for use in the Netherlands East Indies.

Dr. Robert A. Jaffray has instructed his brother to give us a check for an amount sufficient for the purchase of the plane. This amount, according to the best information we have, is $14,163 for the plane laid down in Batavia.

In receiving Mr. Robert A. Jaffray's check from Mr. William G. Jaffray for $14,163, it is understood between us that this money is to be used exclusively for the purchase of the plane and its shipment to Batavia. It is further understood that, if funds come in to our treasury for the plane in the N.E.I. in sufficient amount to cover the requirement of about $2,000 for hangars, about $4,000 for transportation of pilot and family to the field and first year's support on the field, and about $2,500 for operating costs and other expenses - making a total of $8,500, and leave a balance which can be applied toward the purchase of the plane, any such balance will be refunded to Mr. Robert A. Jaffray by check to his account given to his brother as Attorney.

It is further understood that the plane is to be purchased immediately following the receipt of information concerning the Beechcraft plane which will enable us to determine whether to purchase a Waco or a Beechcraft.

On behalf of the Alliance Mr. Snead agrees that the shipment of the plane will not be held up while waiting receipt of money for operating expenses and other needs mentioned above.

A. C. Snead

W. G. Jaffray

A Waco was purchased, the first plane bought by the Alliance. It would be flown in Borneo by George Fisk. Ed Ulrich's Sealand was the fifth plane acquired by the Alliance.

Contents

Foreword

It is a privilege for me to write the foreword to this fascinating book. While I have not had an opportunity to know Ed Ulrich well, I have known of him for most of my adult life.

Ed and his wife Elaine are an important part of a story that ranks as one of the most fascinating, daring and fruitful missionary endeavors ever undertaken. Bringing the gospel, for the first time, to the people of West New Guinea, now called Irian Jaya, was an extraordinary achievement.

Out There Beyond Beyond, based on Ed Ulrich's personal recollections and extensive journals, brings into focus the exceptional courage and faith that was required of all those who were involved in this effort.

As the regional director for East Asia and the Pacific Islands under The Christian and Missionary Alliance, I traveled throughout Irian Jaya on multiple occasions between 1979 and 1991. I had the joy of worshiping in dozens of churches with thousands of believers all over the island. These were experiences that will live with me forever. But on every one of those trips, I was constantly reminded of what it took to give birth to the Church of Jesus Christ in such hostile territory.

The airstrips I landed on so comfortably had required months of backbreaking work to carve out of the jungle. Some of them, built in the 1950s, were only made possible because courageous pioneers were willing to hike for weeks across 14,000-foot-high plateaus and through groups of hostile tribal peoples. The airstrips had to be surveyed, built and then checked out by highly skilled and experienced pilots before any landing could take place.

Ed Ulrich was one of the primary movers in this unique enterprise. He found a way with his colleague and fellow pilot, Al Lewis, to land a seaplane on the Baliem River, making it possible to open the entire area to the gospel. He lived through the stress of a tribal uprising and subsequent massacre of nine people at Obano, and the destruction of the mission plane which had been dedicated just a few days before. Ed lived with the reality that his friend Al Lewis had gone to his death, crashing into a high mountain peak above the entrance to the Baliem Valley. It was a route that Ed himself had flown repeatedly in order to supply the fledgling missionary effort among the Dani people.

Out There Beyond Beyond documents the brief but impressive record of The Christian and Missionary Alliance's involvement in mission aviation. As the first Christian Mission to utilize aircraft to any degree, the Alliance demonstrated a willingness to invest huge sums of money and try unique and innovative methods to further the cause of world evangelization. Ed Ulrich also points out that once having pioneered in this area, the C&MA had the wisdom to turn over the entire aviation program to Mission Aviation Fellowship once MAF became fully operative in Irian Jaya. The Alliance was determined to remain true to its primary calling, which was to evangelism and church planting.

The Christian and Missionary Alliance, the entire missions community and the Christians of Irian Jaya owe a huge debt of gratitude to Ed and Elaine Ulrich for their unswerving commitment to the cause of the gospel. We are also indebted to Ed for preserving for us all this important chapter in the history of Christ's expanding kingdom.

Rev. Peter N. Nanfelt, DD, President
The Christian and Missionary Alliance
Colorado Springs, CO
December 2, 1999

Authors' Note

In one sense, this book is the result of a field trip. One afternoon in 1959, Larry and about four other little boys, then in the elementary grades at the Sentani School, toured the inside of a DC-3 airliner parked at the Sentani airport.

They were met at the airstrip by Captain Ed Ulrich, resplendent in his white uniform and crisp cap. Two of the students, Kenny Troutman and Johnny Cutts, had known Ed just a few years before, when he was "their" pilot who had flown Mission planes their families were dependent on for transportation and supplies. After the tour, Ed came up to Mission Hill to have supper at the school, and the conversation continued for hours. None of the awed boys ever finished writing their report about the field trip, so here it is, forty years later!

This book resulted from the encouragement of many people. The editors of *Flying* magazine in 1958 encouraged Ed's interest in telling this story by publishing an article he sent them. Robert Cowles inspired us with his rousing introduction to Larry's 1979 article in *The Alliance Witness* (now *Alliance Life*) where he described the Baliem Valley entry by the Sealand in 1954 as "probably the most breathless undertaking in all of The Christian and Missionary Alliance's history." And for years, as both Ed and Larry have spoken to church groups, they have heard from many individuals who have been interested in reading more about the pioneering days in New Guinea. Ed was once misintroduced to an Alliance gathering as "a retired MAF pilot," at last prompting this attempt to get something into print about the historic contributions of The Christian and Missionary Alliance to missionary aviation.

Like most memoirs, the book drew on the memories of many people. We would like to thank numerous members of the Alliance family for their assistance in recalling names, dates and incidents, and for giving permission to quote from their letters, books and articles. These include Don and Alice Gibbons, Harold and Mary Catto, Myron and Marjorie Bromley, Ed and Shirley Maxey, Elze Stringer, Fran Bozeman, Dorie Van Stone, Richard Lenehan, Jerry and Darlene Rose, Gordon and Peggy Larson, Bill Nabors, Malcolm and Helen Sawyer, Wayne and Minnie Persons and Alice Mickelson.

Bernard S. King and L.L. King have encouraged Ed's plans for this book for a number of years; both the Kings were instrumental in the development of the work in Netherlands New Guinea. Dr. Joseph Wenninger and his assistants at the Alliance headquarters archives have given valuable help in locating old letters, fund-raising pamphlets and other memorabilia that helped us tell this story. We are thankful for Peter Nanfelt's interest in writing the foreword.

Buzz Maxey and John Cutts, friends of Larry's since grade school days in Sentani, have helped provide up-to-the-minute accounts of life as it is now lived in Irian Jaya, as have Larry's brother Kevin, now a teacher in Sentani, and Paul and Jeannie Burkhart, also on the field.

Fred Lohrer of the Archbold Biological Station, Lake Placid, Florida, and Dr. Guy Musser, Clare Flemming and Pat Brunhauer of the Archbold archives at the American Museum of Natural History have given Larry important assistance in his continuing study of the 1938 discovery of the Baliem Valley and the early years of contact with the Dani. Also invaluable in this regard are Frances Archbold Hufty, sister of Richard Archbold, Jessica Goldstein and Alex Chadwick of National Public Radio and Lowell Thomas, Jr. of Anchorage, Alaska.

MAF pilots George Boggs, Dave Wunsch, Perry Pust, Len Van Wingerden and Dave Steiger have helped us tell the story of missionary airplanes in New Guinea; Janet Steiger offered use of parts of her book, *Wings over Shangri-la,* for enhancing our own.

For special editorial assistance we are grateful to Christian Publications editor Marilynne Foster, to Elaine Ulrich, to Myron and Marjorie Bromley and to Nance McCown. Any mistakes that have lurked undetected did so despite the best efforts of these indefatigable readers and enthusiasts for the English language, and despite our efforts too.

Any book written nearly fifty years after the events described runs the risk of containing archaic references and anachronistic terminology. For example, in the space of less than ten years, one town mentioned in this book had four different names! To simplify matters, we have "frozen" most references to the year 1954. Then, rain forests were still jungles and wetlands were swamps, and the people we now call Ekari or Me were known as Kapauku. One 1954 custom we *have* abandoned is the use of the word "native" as a noun. If you see the word "native" here, it will be an adjective.

In 1954 the Baliem Valley was in Netherlands New Guinea, so we refer to it that way here, although some of the narrative covers the political events when it became Irian Jaya, a province of Indonesia. (To illustrate this issue of change, one should note that at this writing, Irian Jaya is scheduled to become three provinces.) And in 1954, the seaport near Sentani was Hollandia. Only a few years later, it would be called Kota Baru, then Sukarnapura. Now it is Jayapura.

To simplify reading, and to promote linguistic accuracy (with thanks to Myron Bromley), we have resisted the English practice of adding an "s" to the names of indigenous groups, and instead refer to a group of Baliem people as Dani, not Danis. The same practice is followed with the Kapauku, Moni and other groups.

Ed would like to thank his wife Elaine to whom he owes the utmost thanks for her support and encouragement. Despite all the suspense and uncertainty associated with the hazards of Ed's flying over dangerous terrain and in unfavorable weather, she remained cheerful, optimistic and prayerful. They are best friends and are grateful for the years that God has given them together.

Larry is indebted to those who have made his various trips to Irian Jaya possible. He is thankful to his parents Hi and Mary Lake, Alliance missionaries in the Baliem Valley from 1957 to 1965, for taking him there in the first place. He thanks Mission Aviation Fellowship, Summer Institute of Linguistics, Messiah College and numerous churches and individuals for helping fund and expedite his Irian Jaya research trips in 1979, 1987, 1992-1993 and 1995. He is particularly thankful for Mary Beth's loving patience with the travels and customs of "Island Boy," and to Nick and Maggie for their cheerfulness as participant observers on several Irian Jaya trips, and, more recently, their giving up some of their time at the family computer so this book could be completed.

Captain Edward W. Ulrich
Sharon, Pennsylvania
Dr. Larry M. Lake
Camp Hill, Pennsylvania

1

God's Invasion

One Tuesday morning, many years ago, I sat in the cockpit of a small British-made seaplane and looked out on a world that few had ever seen. Several thousand feet below were twisting white-water streams draining the high mountains that rose, dark and cloud-covered, on either side.

Behind me, in the distance, flowed the Idenburg River, where these streams eventually emptied. The Idenburg, as slow and sinuous and muddy brown as a lazy snake, wound its ancient way north to the Pacific Ocean. Looking to the west, I could see row upon row of high mountain ranges, virtually unexplored, a physical and psychological barrier to what was commonly known as the civilized world, a barrier that had kept out almost all outside influences for thousands of years.

These were the central ranges of the island of New Guinea, the largest tropical island in the world. On a map, it stretches like a 1,500-mile-long bird in the south Pacific Ocean just north of Australia. At that time, the eastern half of the island was administered by Australia and would someday become independent Papua New Guinea.

The western half, over which the seaplane now flew, was Netherlands New Guinea (now Irian Jaya), the last vestige of what had once been an enormous colonial empire stretching over 3,500 miles from the tip of Sumatra to the southeastern corner of west New Guinea, commanding the sea routes near the Spice Islands. In the twentieth century, early in the ministry of The Christian and Missionary Alliance, those islands of Indonesia had already become a significant mission field.

To my left in the plane was Al Lewis, veteran of missionary flying on another island, Kalimantan, then known as Borneo. We were the two pilots assigned to the Aviation Section of the Netherlands New Guinea field of The Christian and Missionary Alliance. Together with Al, a few months earlier, I had flown this plane 12,000 miles from the Short Brothers and Harland factory in Belfast, Northern Ireland. It had been a journey of twenty-two days including mechanical delays, eighty-six hours of flying, difficult navigational problems and bad weather—a long journey with stops in seventeen countries.

But in many ways, today's journey, only 150 miles, was longer and more monumental still. Today's flight was the culmination of a vision that God had given Alliance statesman Robert A. Jaffray seventeen years before as he worked and prayed and planned at the Mission's Bible school in Makassar, a city on the island of Sulawesi, then known as Celebes. Dr. Jaffray had seen a vision of a vast host of people in the mountains of Dutch New Guinea crying out for the gospel. He had heard of a pilot's discovery of the Wissel Lakes in 1936, but some aspects of his vision were far more encompassing than just that area of New Guinea.

In the Mission's field publication, *The Pioneer,* in July 1938, he wrote:

> How do we reach them? We do not know, but we are sure that we will never find out by sitting here in Makassar. We feel an urge to go and see what can be done. These people are included in the "every creature" of my commission. If men after gold and oil may go, why not the missionary seeking precious souls, even though he may have to fly to them?

A year after Jaffray's vision, and even as the issue of *The Pioneer* was going to press, an American millionaire explorer/biologist, flying his expedition's seaplane from his base on the north coast of New Guinea, looked out of his cockpit window to find grass-thatched villages in a broad valley far below. Until then, the highland populations of this part of New Guinea had been unknown to most of the outside world, except to visionaries like Robert Jaffray. The valley that the explorer Richard Archbold saw was the Grand Valley of the Baliem River. Even then Archbold was aware of the significance of finding a large population in interior New Guinea and wrote in a *National Geographic* article:

> We made our first reconnaissance flight on June 21, but clouds lying over the lowlands prevented us from getting a clear picture of what lay below. The next two flights, however, brought astonishing discoveries. Between the Idenburg and Lake Habbema we flew over an unmapped valley of the Baliem River perhaps 10 miles wide by 40 miles long.
>
> From the number of gardens and stockaded villages composed of groups of round houses roofed with domes of grass thatch, we estimated the population to be at least 60,000. Subsequent meetings with many of the people convinced us that we were the first white men ever to penetrate their isolated domain.

From then on, missionaries and members of The Christian and Missionary Alliance gazed at Archbold's pictures of the Dani, of garden fences and of the tree-lined Baliem in that *National Geographic* article and prayed that the gospel would come soon to the Baliem Valley.

Those prayers continued through the years of World War II, when sightseeing military personnel flying over the valley gave it the name Shangri-la. Those prayers continued during the difficult postwar years of Indonesia's independence movement which distracted the attention of the Netherlands government for a time from further pursuits in New Guinea. Those prayers continued during years of preparation and planning by Alliance missionaries.

Today's flight was an answer to those prayers. Al Lewis and I, Ed Ulrich, missionaries with The Christian and Missionary Alliance, and two of our missionary colleagues, were about to land in Shangri-la for the very first time.

Months before, at a dedication service at the Belfast factory, our Sealand airplane had been christened *The Gospel Messenger.* Now I looked over my shoulder and through the little passageway to the cabin. Somewhat incongruously, the bulkhead was made of polished wood paneling, more suitable for the private air yacht of a wealthy industrialist than a tool of the kingdom of God.

For years, perhaps out of habit from the war years or perhaps out of respect for the Bible's spiritual warfare metaphors, we had talked and prayed about the Baliem entry in terms of "invasion," of "establishing a beachhead," of being "God's invasion force." In the cabin were the members of our invasion force: four adults and a baby—Einar Mickelson, Lloyd Van Stone and Elisa and Ruth Gobai and their baby daughter,

Dorcas, a Christian family from the Kapauku group 200 miles to the west of the Baliem.

Members of our Mission team had some knowledge of social behavior from years of living and working with people in other parts of New Guinea's highlands. We knew that the presence of women in the company of warriors often indicated to others their peaceful intentions, enabling them to move about through dangerous territory. It was for this reason that we had invited the Gobai family to accompany us on this flight. We sincerely hoped that the people of the Baliem would respect this custom.

Packed into the cabin around and behind and in the aisle were 500 pounds of cargo: two tents, two sleeping bags, lanterns, a radio, batteries, an ax, eighty-nine pounds of food supplies, and pressurized camping stoves. Other equipment included four cameras (two of them 16mm movie cameras), fourteen pounds of medical supplies, two twelve-gauge shotguns with cartridges for hunting small game, seventy-three pounds of personal effects including clothing, papers, books, Bibles and writing supplies, and a supply of cowrie shells, beads and knives to be used for trading with the Dani people the team hoped to befriend.

Mr. Mickelson had planned the supplies so that the party could survive in the Baliem for a month in the event that we could not get back to pick them up before then. We would leave them in the valley this morning, and then, if the weather was good, return with another load of cargo later that day.

It was a typical rainy-season morning with low clouds and moderate precipitation. Our flight to the Baliem from our Sentani base (officially known as Hollandia by the airport control tower, named for the nearby capital city of Netherlands New Guinea) was over 150 miles of unexplored jungle usually hidden under layers of cloud and lines of thunderstorms. When we could see the trees, they were vague smudges of dark green.

Imagine a million square miles of broccoli tops partly hidden by the cottony fluff of clouds—that is what the New Guinea jungles looked like from our cockpit. Here and there, especially in the more swampy areas around Sentani Lake, lighter green asterisks punctuated the dark carpet. These were sago palms, a tree whose inner starch is used for food by many of the lowland peoples of New Guinea and other areas of the Pacific.

With today's cloudy weather, the jungle appeared below us only in small patches, not the breathtaking expanse we would see on clearer days. Where the lower jungles ended, the mountains rose to 14,000 feet and completely surrounded our destination.

We had planned to take off from Sentani at 7:30 a.m. so that we could reach the mountains early and slip through the narrow pass at 9,000 feet before cumulus buildups covered the ranges. But because of the poor weather at

Sentani, we'd delayed our departure almost two hours. Accurate weather reporting was still far in New Guinea's future.

With the Sentani weather improving, we pulled out onto the runway and departed for what we hoped would be our first landing in the Baliem. The twin-engine Short Sealand amphibian easily topped the cloud layers at 11,500 feet. It was still raining up there from a higher overcast, but for the six aboard, it was a bright day of which some of us had dreamed for fifteen years.

It had often seemed that it might never come, especially while we were raising the $130,000 for the plane plus thousands more for spare parts. The 1990s equivalent of that amount in 1950 dollars is now over $2 million.

Even the decision to spend that money on this plane rather than on some other aircraft had been a long and difficult one. Some missionaries had suggested that we buy a costly but powerful Catalina seaplane similar to the one so successfully used by Archbold. His was powered by two radial engines producing 900 horsepower each, and weighed over 25,000 pounds when fully loaded with 7,000 pounds of cargo, fuel and personnel. But even military surplus models of the Catalinas were three or four times more expensive than a new Sealand.

Other airplanes we considered were smaller. One of these was the Grumman Goose, an American seaplane similar in size to the Short Sealand Al had flown in Borneo. For the kinds of tasks we expected of the airplane, it finally seemed that the Sealand would be the least expensive choice. It was categorized as a light plane (gross weight of 10,500 pounds or less). Its wing-span was sixty-one feet (compared to the 104 feet of Archbold's plane), forty-two feet from nose to tail. It could carry eight passengers.

After the Mission decided on the aircraft, the order was made and the company began building the plane. Unlike mass-produced cars and other items, most aircraft are built for a specific customer, even though they are constructed on assembly lines in factories. (The per-unit cost of building them is too high for a manufacturer to absorb without having a paid customer signed up.) So the wait was long even after the order had been placed.

This day had looked closer only when we took delivery of the plane in Belfast and started for New Guinea, half a world away.

Now having flown for an hour, it was not safe to continue any longer at 11,500 feet because we still could not see the mountains we knew were almost upon us. Would we have to turn back, or would the curtain lift so we could enter the pass?

We tried a few circles. After all, the weather changes rapidly in New Guinea, and a circle or two could buy us a little time and perhaps a chance at finding a break in the clouds. Finally, we spotted a faint line of crags. Then, after a few more circles, Al straightened up the plane and aimed it for the valley. We slipped across the ridge.

Just one hour and five minutes after takeoff we entered the Baliem Valley. It was a bright day there. Heavy clouds had built up on the outer sides of the mountains, leaving the ten-by-forty-mile valley quite clear. We made a shallow turn to the left. Since we were still flying at 11,000 feet, and the Baliem Valley and its river were just over 5,000 feet above sea level, we needed to lose some altitude before setting up our landing.

As we cleared the mountains, Al raised his right hand to the throttle array on the ceiling and pulled back on the two ivory-colored plastic knobs that controlled our engines. As he reduced the power, the roar of the engines diminished. Our ears felt "pinched" as they reacted to the loss in altitude. Al adjusted the flaps, the large panels in the trailing edge of the wings that would reduce our speed and help us land more slowly.

Following our landing checklist, we changed the propeller and fuel mixture settings. Al checked the small panel near his right knee. Three small red lights glowed there, telling us that all three wheels were up, tucked in their positions inside the hull. We would not need those wheels until our return to Sentani.

We all leaned toward the windows, eyes wide to see the vast Grand Valley of the Baliem River. As the plane slowed down, we began to feel more of the bumps in the airstream, mild bounces caused by air rising from some features on the ground and sinking over others.

Deep green forests covered the mountains and high hills surrounding the valley, but the floor of the valley was predominantly light green. Sunlight winked at us from carefully laid-out garden drainage ditches full of muddy water. Sweet potato plants sprawled their green leafy vines over the rich brown earth of the gardens. Here and there in the valley were tall stands of evergreen trees, some of them sheltering villages.

Dani villages consist of groups of light brown thatched-roofed round houses joined together by wooden fences topped with more brown-grass thatching. From the air, the round houses looked like mushrooms. Along one side of a village were several longer houses used by women for cooking and for shelter from sun and rain. We could see bluish-gray smoke oozing through the thatch. It was just past breakfast time in the Baliem Valley.

As we lost more altitude, we could see people working in gardens drained by an elaborate system of ditches. We flew over the gently winding Baliem River, its light-brown water flowing between dark gray mud banks covered by a thick growth of evergreen trees. These were casuarina trees, named long ago by scientists because of the resemblance of the tree's needles to the feathers of the cassowary, New Guinea's large flightless bird, similar to an ostrich. The Baliem, bordered by casuarinas, meanders near the center of the long valley.

Our destination was a short stretch of the river at the southern end of the valley. During a survey flight, we had picked out this stretch as the most suitable place for a landing. We had particularly chosen this month of April for our initial invasion of the valley since it was at the middle of the rainy season; the river should be at its highest level and remain so for at least three months.

We circled lower and lower over the river. Al and I made some careful checks of our location, of the appearance of the river, of the operation of the airplane. Everything had to be right. Because of our load, our altitude and the high hills ahead of us, we would not be able to make a "go around." It was land or crash!

At higher altitudes, airplanes' wings and engines cannot do the work they can do at sea level. Once we touched the water, we could not change our minds: we would not be able to fly off the river with our present load once we slowed down in the water. Flying can be an exacting science!

The Baliem River offered few straight stretches. It was in flood and flowing very swiftly. Suddenly, during what we hoped would be our last circle as we lined up for the landing, we saw arrows rising from a village beside us. The Dani were shooting at us! Were they just having some fun with the "big bird," or were they being hostile toward us?

Earlier that morning, before takeoff at Sentani, we had prayed for our safety and that of the plane. We had prayed for the Dani and for a friendly reception. Now they were using us for target practice!

We made another circle.

We prayed again.

It was time to land in the Baliem.

We began letting down over the river. The overhanging branches of trees on the riverbank appeared close, but we thought the wing tips would clear them. Al and I made a final cockpit check: the flaps were at the correct angle, three red lights showing the wheels were up, propellers were adjusted for a landing. Al reached up again and pulled the throttles back a little more.

In these last few seconds of the flight, we broadcast a series of terse reports of the landing to the folks listening so carefully to the radio at the Sentani base:

"Turning onto final approach."

"A slight turn to the right to follow the river."

"We are below the tops of the trees."

"Now below the brush on the banks."

"We're on the water!"

"Hallelujah!"

Landing against the eight-to-ten-knot current slowed us down very quickly. The river was even higher than we had expected it to be. Although we had planned to put our party out on the east bank, we were unable to get close enough because the trees on that side were hanging over the river. Those gray-green casuarina trees which had looked so lacy and graceful from the air were now formidable obstacles with thick, gnarled trunks and wide-spreading branches that seemed to be reaching out to devour the plane.

With propellers in reverse, we eased out into the center of the stream and drifted slowly backward down-current looking for other possibilities. When a likely place caught our eye, Al took the propellers out of reverse mode and used the thrust to hold the plane stationary against the current. We could feel the hull bobbing up and down in the water.

A section of bank on the west side of the river looked promising except for a patch of tall reeds extending some twenty-five feet out into the water. We quickly discussed our options and decided to take the plane into the bank among the reeds.

As Al guided us, there was a terrific chatter against the roof and side of the plane: the propellers were cutting into the cane, and debris was flying back at us. After some skillful maneuvering and more of the unsettling noise, Al floated the plane near the bank and shut down both engines.

The racket was replaced by the sounds of tall grasses scraping against the skin and water slapping against the hull. We cut off the switches, resetting some controls so that we could take off quickly once we unloaded passengers and supplies.

As soon as we were settled in the water, I crawled out through the cockpit's large side window to tie a fifty-foot rope to the nose of the plane. The area just in front of the windshield was painted in a flat black slip-resistant paint. It felt rough on my hands as I positioned myself to slide into the water. Hoping to get a good footing, I was surprised when I could not reach bottom.

I grasped the reeds and pulled myself toward shallower water near the bank. Wet, cold, muddy and breathless, I struggled to grip the slippery mud bank and be the first one of our party actually to set foot in the Baliem Valley. I soon discovered that the rope was not long enough to reach the tree I was heading for. I called to Lloyd. He found another fifty-foot length, and we managed to secure the plane.

Were the Dani nearby? Would we be attacked? Would it be over quickly? Or would they wait and ambush us later? We knew little about these people. No outsider had contacted them for more than fifteen years.

2

Smuggled to New Guinea

The Baliem Valley was a long way from my childhood roots in Western Pennsylvania. I was born in Pittsburgh on June 2, 1922. When I was two years old, my parents moved to Sharon, Pennsylvania, a small blue-collar town near the Ohio border. My father worked for Westinghouse for over thirty-five years as an electrical engineer and foreman.

Like many kids, I went through the model airplane stage, building models out of balsa wood frames covered with tissue paper. As early as I can remember, I was excited about the idea of flying. Over the years, this finally led to the actual thrill of learning to fly. I took my first flying lessons at a small airstrip in Greenville, not far from my home.

The United States entered World War II the winter after I graduated from Sharon High School. At age nineteen, I enlisted in the Army Air Corps where I was commissioned a second lieutenant. After the war, the Army Air Corps would become the United States Air Force. My first phase of flight training was at Spartan Air College in Tulsa, Oklahoma.

When I graduated in April, 1943, I was assigned as an instructor. Soon I was at Del Rio, Texas, training flight crews in the Martin B-26 "Marauder," a newly designed two-engine attack bomber. It had received a reputation as a "hot" airplane—meaning fast and hard to control. It deserved its reputation. Very fast in flight, it also had an unusually high approach speed; the pilot would have to maintain almost 130 miles per hour until just before touching the runway for a landing. (Jet airliners now sometimes have approach speeds a little higher than that; but for that time, when the DC-3 had an approach speed of seventy mph, and the Piper Cubs about fifty-five, the B-26 was a hot airplane indeed.)

I taught hundreds of pilots on the B-26, and many of them served in the memorable air war in both the Pacific and European theaters. In 1943, in fact, the B-26 became the most important element in the air war against Japanese shipping in the Pacific. Although it was land-based, it was often used on long over-water missions to attack sea targets.

Even though its manufacturer gave it the warlike name "Marauder," the B-26 soon had acquired some less desirable nicknames, including "Flying Coffin," "One-a-Day in Tampa Bay" and "Widow Maker."

Typically, missionary aviation in the 1950s would involve small single-engine airplanes. But during my military experience I had learned to fly multi-engine airplanes with much more complicated systems. Years later, in New Guinea, I would find that my experience in multi-engine aircraft had prepared me for the specialized flying that was involved.

In 1945, I was assigned to a B-24 training program in Smyrna, Tennessee. The B-24 "Liberator" was a huge, four-engine bomber with twin tails, nicknamed "The Flying Boxcar" for its squarish shape. Every day I conducted training missions over the wooded hills of eastern Tennessee.

Not all the flying in the war was bomber or fighter flying, of course. To support troops located in all corners of the earth, the Allies relied on former airline pilots and others to operate the equivalent of a super-airline responsible for transporting vital supplies and key personnel. Consequently, many of us were given the opportunity to obtain an ATR license, the Air Transport Rating that would provide airline jobs later. I could not know at that time that, in the years to come, having such a license would give me opportunities to fly in some of the most remote parts of the world.

Each country has its own examinations and requirements for the Air Transport Rating. By the time I retired with over 20,000 hours of flying, I would have the ATR from Indonesia, China and the Netherlands, as well as from the United States. This would allow me to transition quickly to a local airline in New Guinea when the Alliance's flying days were over, and later to obtain commercial flying jobs in the United States and subsequently in Southeast Asia. But more about that later.

As the war progressed, more bomber designs were produced, culminating in the Boeing B-29 Stratofortress, the type that dropped nuclear weapons on Japan. Of course, each new aircraft type required appropriate training programs for flight and maintenance crews. Just before the war ended, I was selected as an instructor for the B-29 crews, but did not proceed to teach. At the end of the war, I was a first lieutenant.

In 1948, my wife Alberta, to whom I had been married six and a half years, died of Bright's disease, a kidney infection. Our son, Ted, was only five at the time. Just before she was diagnosed, I received the Lord under the ministry of Rev. Harold J. Sutton, pastor of the Meadville Alliance Church. Knowing the Lord during that stressful time gave me hope that our lives were truly in God's hands.

As the disease progressed, my wife became so ill that she was eventually confined to the hospital. Before she died, I had the privilege of leading her to the Lord. These were painful and difficult months for our family, yet God sustained us.

I continued to attend the Meadville church and, after several months, met Elaine, Pastor Sutton's daughter, who had come home from St. Paul Bible College (now Crown College). Although I was somewhat intimidated by the Suttons' position and reputation, as I courted their daughter I found that they were gracious, warm-hearted and good-humored people. Elaine and I were married in August, 1949, a year and a half after Alberta's death.

A year later, sensing a call to some form of ministry, I applied to enter the theological studies program at St. Paul. During registration, Rev. Harry L. Turner, the dean, called me out of the line and asked if I would consider missionary service as a pilot with the Alliance. I accepted the offer as a confirmation of the Lord's call on my life and my intention to dedicate myself to His service.

Before I finished my first year of studies, we received our appointment to Indonesia. I was to become part of a support team supplying aviation services to the missionaries in Borneo. That air service, the first operated by any Mission organization, had been started in 1938 by pilot George Fisk and continued by Fred Jackson. The first plane, a Beechcraft on floats, was intentionally destroyed during the war so it would not fall into the hands of the Japanese.

After the war, the Alliance established air service in Borneo with Al Lewis as pilot. It was hoped that one aircraft could serve both the Borneo and New Guinea fields. However, the Indonesian war for independence, beginning in 1945 and ending with the Dutch recognizing the independence of Indonesia in August 1949, soon put an end to those plans.

Although there was no airplane there at the time, we were sent to Indonesia anyway. Since we needed to study the Indonesian language before we would be fully useful in ministry, it seemed best to start right away.

On March 29, 1952, Elaine, Ted and I said good-bye to our families and boarded a ship in New York harbor, destination—Makassar, an ancient southeast Asian seaport on the sprawling island of Sulawesi, where we would begin language study. Since the 1920s, the Alliance had had a Mission base at Makassar. It was there that Dr. Robert Jaffray developed a thriving Bible school for Indonesian Christians and launched the outreach in New Guinea. In fact, it was from Makassar that Walter Post and Russell Deibler established the Mission's station at Enarotali in the Wissel Lakes in 1939.

Makassar, later known as Ujung Pandang, was a commercial and transportation hub for the eastern part of Indonesia. It was well located to serve the logistical needs of aviator, merchant, seaman, naturalist and missionary alike. Within an hour of our arrival in Makassar, Walter Post informed us that we would begin language study in five days!

Our outfit arrived safely—and on the same ship we had been on! That was a miracle in itself. After almost two weeks of visits to the seaport warehouse, discussions with officials and pages and pages of cargo manifests, we were most grateful when we were charged a flat one percent duty amounting to less than $12.

Life in Makassar was certainly different from life in the United States. We lived in the Mission headquarters with the Brills and Posts. Our neighbors bathed at a common well in the neighborhood and kept their chickens, ducks and other livestock under their houses. It was a crowded, smelly, noisy place, but an excellent environment in which to learn a new language.

Indonesian roosters don't seem to know that they are supposed to crow at sunrise, not all night long! And with thin-walled houses so closely built to each other, we smelled our neighbors' food and heard their singing and conversation at almost all hours. And five times a day we heard the wail of the Muslim call to prayer broadcast through loudspeakers from small mosques throughout the city.

We arrived in Makassar during the "cooler" season, but as far as we were concerned, it was hot enough already. The temperature was typically in the high 80s by mid-morning and even higher by the afternoon. We found that the days just kept getting hotter as the year progressed. Then, in November, the rainy season began, bringing more discomfort because of the high humidity. This was not the weather of Sharon, Pennsylvania.

Ted was in fourth grade. His homeschooling with the Calvert method and Elaine's able teaching progressed smoothly in this strange environment. The missionary children's school at Makassar had not yet reopened after Indonesia's four-year war for independence from the Dutch. Although that war had ended with the Dutch departure from their former colony in 1949, tensions in the newly independent nation were still high, and suspicions of the motives of foreigners like us were plentiful. Elaine recalls an unpleasant but humorous encounter with the Indonesian authorities:

> I was teaching our nine-year-old son Ted, using the Calvert system. One morning while we were "in school," an Indonesian office worker delivered a summons to me from the police. *What have I done?* I wondered. I didn't drive. I seldom left the compound. I had a valid visa. I couldn't imagine what offense I had committed. One of the mission staff told me how to get to the police station, and I set off alone in a *tiga roda* (a bicycle-rickshaw type of vehicle).
>
> My inquisitor's knowledge of English matched my knowledge of Indonesian—the minimum! Finally I understood that my "crime" was that I had sent a check to

the Calvert School to pay for Ted's books and supplies. Why that was a crime took a long time for the officer to explain and for me to understand.

"It is not permitted to send money out of Indonesia," he said.

Oh, I thought, *I can explain that—maybe!*

Before I could begin, the questions came:

"What was this money for?"

"For my son's school books."

"Why do you need to have these books?"

"So I can teach him."

"Why can't he go to the Indonesian school?"

"Because he doesn't know the language; and besides, we're not going to be here very long." (Bad mistake on my part, like waving a red flag.)

"Oh? And where are you going?"

"We're going to be sent out of Makassar."

The next questions focused on my having sent money out of the country. I tried to explain that the check was written on an American bank, for American money. "But sir, this money was never in Indonesia."

"You must not send money out of Indonesia!"

"The money never was *in* Indonesia."

"Look! Here is the check; here is the envelope you mailed it in. You *were* sending money out of Indonesia."

We were at an impasse. I was dismissed abruptly, curtly, with the declaration that the police would send for me again.

They did—the next week. The setting was the same, only the interrogator was a different officer. We went over the same ground. The officer was skeptical. He demanded proof that we had such a bank account in the States and ordered me to bring my bank book so that he could see how much money we had.

When I replied that I couldn't do that, he sent me away with the threat that the next time I would have to have better answers.

Another week passed. Another summons came.

This time I went to another location, to an officer who questioned me in English. The questions followed the same line; I gave the same answers. Seemingly exasperated, the officer told me that my next appearance would be before the judge. Then, with a pointed look at my middle (I was eight months pregnant), he sneered, "And if you have to go to jail, it will be very bad for you."

Before I could stop myself, I blurted out, "It would be very bad for you too!"

I heard no more from the Indonesian police.

Such encounters and the dozens of daily interactions with neighbors produced considerable strain. Living and working in another culture is a very difficult undertaking. Yet even in the earliest days in Makassar, God developed in both of us a love for the cross-cultural life that would last for years to come.

At conference that year, we were appointed to four more months of language study in Makassar, not because we were doing badly, but because the Board of Managers in New York would consider the decision for a new plane for Borneo in their September meeting. At that point, there was a possibility that two planes would be bought, one for Borneo, for which I would be responsible, and one for New Guinea, which would be Al Lewis' responsibility. However, only one plane was purchased. It would be based in New Guinea, and both we and the Lewises would be assigned there.

The birth of our daughter Lynne in April, 1953, delighted us, but presented us with unanticipated political problems. I traveled to Jakarta to register her birth with the American Embassy and secured documentary proof of her American citizenship. By the time she was a month old, we were in the process of securing exit permits from authorities in Makassar for our move to New Guinea. They refused permission for baby Lynne.

"She is a citizen of Indonesia; she can't go."

"No, she's an American citizen; here is her certificate."

"No, she is an Indonesian; you will have to leave her here."

"With whom?"

"With the head of your Mission."

Not likely!

This conversation was repeated in three offices, and at last, we simply gave up.

When the sailing date arrived, Lynne was six weeks old. The Brills helped us carry our baggage on board the small ship, including a gently carried laundry basket. A simple blanket was draped over it.

That basket contained our most precious cargo, Lynne!

3

Life on Mission Hill

The town of Sentani, located on the shores of beautiful Lake Sentani, was at that time the headquarters town for all Mission activity in New Guinea. A rather spartan place, it had once been just a tiny fishing village until the Japanese occupation of the island. Eventually it would become the home of three air bases.

When General Douglas MacArthur led Allied forces in reclaiming the nearby colonial port city of Hollandia (now Jayapura) in April, 1944, a major objective was occupation of the entire coastal area for use as an enormous military base. It would be a staging area for the eventual reclamation of the Philippines and for the closing stages of the war.

For a time, Sentani became the headquarters for General MacArthur, who even had a large house built which he named "The White House." All that remains of that edifice, and of

MacArthur's presidential aspirations, is a concrete slab overlooking Lake Sentani.

Concrete slabs, in fact, were one of the more useful legacies of the war years in Sentani. Ultimately, most of the aluminum-walled missionary homes built on Mission Hill, used old army slabs as their foundations.

Another legacy was the harrowing blacktop road which wound its twenty miles of hairpin curves between the port of Hollandia and Sentani.

After the war years, the air bases at Sentani deteriorated, and eventually only one was in regular operation. It had originally been called Sentani Airstrip. The name stuck, although by the '70s it would acquire the grand name of Sentani International Airport. Still with a single runway, at least it had been improved by lengthening and the addition of lighting equipment for night landings.

When we first started using Sentani as our base, the airport tower was an old portable control tower from the war which had been parked in a lawn area between the main ramp and the runway. Only in the late '50s was this replaced by a terminal building complete with concrete tower and a wing to house the meteorology department. (In the early '90s, the terminal complex was expanded to support increased passenger traffic, including two daily flights to Indonesia's capital, Jakarta.)

In the grassy plains just to the west of Sentani Airstrip was another decaying war base, known in our time simply as "The Old Airstrip," but once known as "Cyclops Airdrome," named after the imposing 7,000-foot mountain which rose behind Mission Hill. In many places in the tall weeds of the old airstrip one could find wrecked parts of old warplanes, many of them the Japanese fighter bombers that were destroyed in the first attacks from the U.S. Navy's carrier *Enterprise* in 1944. For many years, pilots and mechanics, not to mention school children, scrounged among these old wrecks for useful hardware or interesting curiosities.

In contrast to the blue, heavily jungled Cyclops Mountain, the rounded hills near Sentani Lake were thickly carpeted in a coarse tall grass, broken sometimes by small copses of dark trees.

Once the decision was made to purchase a plane, it became a necessity to provide a shelter for it. An aluminum aircraft can corrode badly in such a climate if its skin is not protected well. The maintenance crew would also need a dry and shaded place in the hot and humid climate.

Through our contacts in Australia, we located a firm that built prefabricated buildings. So, in June 1953, I left for Australia aboard a KLM flight to complete the hangar purchase.

The sheet metal building I chose didn't look like much more than a pile of steel struts and corrugated sheets at that time. This material was shipped to Papua New Guinea, and then, by special arrangements with the Dutch government, to Hollandia harbor, where it was loaded onto trucks and driven on the winding, crumbling, war-vintage blacktop road out to the airport.

Our early plans did not include a concrete floor for the hangar, so it was gravel. Because of the hangar's ample size, the Mission's Dodge Fargo pickup truck and other vehicles could be driven into it out of the tropical afternoon rains, and the cargo could be loaded directly into the plane.

Meanwhile, up the road at Mission Hill, our first simple accommodations in the old mess hall were shared with other missionary families. Elaine has some vivid memories of those days:

> Life in the old U.S. Army building was challenging and exciting. Jerry and Darlene Rose, Einar Mickelson, Lloyd and Doris Van Stone and their two children, and our family of four lived in the "mess." Al and Mary were sleeping in their own home, although it was still unfinished. We all ate dinner together. Mary and I took turns cooking.
>
> Huge Norway rats plagued our existence. They ran back and forth above us on the sagging canvas ceilings. While we sat at dinner one evening, Ed shot a rat as it ran behind the stove. They also ate through the plastic screen in the cupboard and ruined two beautiful apple pies I had made (with carefully hoarded dried apples) to celebrate Ed's return from the hangar-buying trip to Australia.

Ed's first project was to replace the plastic in Lynne's screened-in crib with wire screen!

On a ridge overlooking the town, the airstrip and Sentani Lake, the missionary team constructed a community of wood-frame houses with corrugated aluminum walls and roofs with extensive overhangs. Each house, used in later years for the Sentani School, had two bedrooms, a large living and dining area, kitchen and bathroom. The window openings had no glass, but were covered only with screen.

We reclaimed a water pipeline constructed of six-inch steel pipe once used by the military. The water, from a mountain stream, was very cold, but we designed our own hot water system—a hose coiled on the roof where the tropical sun would supply the heat.

In a large shed across the dirt road from our house was the Mission's one-cylinder generator with a five-foot diameter flywheel. Once this was cranked into motion—and it didn't always cooperate—we enjoyed electricity for four hours each evening. Otherwise our light came from kerosene lamps.

A little bit of landscaping helped bring a touch of home to Mission Hill. Mr. Mickelson, (whom we all called Mr. Mike) planted several hundred evergreen trees, and in each yard we cultivated bushes and flowers that would grow well—poinsettias, hibiscus, yellow allamandas at the Lewises', pink zinnias at our house, Mrs.

Mike's purple snapdragons further up the hill, and a hedge of colorful crotons at the Lenehans' house nearest the mess hall.

Elaine wrote:

> I loved life at Sentani. Our house was at the base of 7,000-foot Mt. Cyclops. Ever-changing light and shadows played across the mountain. At night, a cooling breeze flowed down the slopes, bringing relief from the day's torrid heat. Psalm 121:1-2 took on a special meaning for me: "I will lift up mine eyes unto the hills, from whence cometh my help. My help cometh from the LORD, which made heaven and earth."

But establishing a home in the tropics was not just about tropical fruits, beautiful flowers and pleasant views. Just as our house was completed, Elaine and I both came down with severe cases of malaria, the mosquito-borne disease that plagues tropic-dwellers. We were in bed for several days, suffering from chills and very high fevers. I was still not fully recovered when I departed for Belfast, Ireland to pick up the Sealand.

Not yet well herself, Elaine recorded her own struggle during those days:

> The night that Ed left, I awoke to see something on my bed. As I shined the flashlight, a big rat jumped off and ran into the closet. The next day, Mr. Mike

helped me put up a mosquito net to prevent my being bitten by mosquitos that could carry malaria from me to the children. The net would also keep the rats out. I went to bed feeling quite safe.

In the middle of the night, I awoke to see a rat running down from the partition along the tape that tied the net, and down the net itself! I thought of the holes in the plastic screen, and I knew that mosquito netting would offer little resistance to a determined rat. Ted had a net, but would he be safe?

My fear began to look like a phobia. Still weak from the malaria, I was easy prey for discouragement. I read by the Aladdin lamplight until the middle of the night, seeking comfort in Scripture. At last, I came to find not only comfort, but what became for me a command—Psalm 91:5a: "Thou shalt not be afraid for the terror by night."

"O Lord," I prayed, "You know that these rats are a terror by night. I believe You are commanding me not to be afraid, as well as promising me that I do not need to be afraid."

The Lord dealt with my fears; the open places in the house were enclosed, and seldom did a rat get in from then on.

Life at Sentani was good, the Mission community loving and supportive. While Al and I were in Ireland, they were particularly helpful to our wives, and the days settled into a routine of housework, child care and homeschooling. Although our area was officially the territory of the Dutch Reformed Church, the women were allowed to have Bible studies with their Indonesian counterparts.

"Difficult challenges in a beautiful setting." That phrase truly described Mission Hill. It was there that much of the praying and planning took place that led to the mighty expansion of God's kingdom into the long-unreachable highlands of Netherlands New Guinea.

4

Around the World in Eighteen Days

Prior to the purchase by the Alliance of their first Sealand, which Al had flown in Borneo, the Mission carefully researched their options. This time too they settled on another Sealand, a small amphibian designed specifically for use in the difficult flying conditions of third world countries. Though we would not take delivery of the plane until late November, I landed in the British Isles on September 25, 1953. Al, who had arrived earlier, met me at the terminal in London. We then proceeded to Belfast, Ireland to the Short Brothers and Harland plant.

At a cavernous factory, which a few years earlier had bustled with the assembly of World War II flying boats, workers in gray overalls were now building airplanes for more peaceful uses. The piercing sounds of rivets being driven into aluminum alternated with the hissing of sprayed paint and the hammering of hydraulic presses shaping aluminum parts. Small cranes suspended on overhead tracks helped move sub-assemblies into place. Numbers painted on the floor oriented workers to their location, and announcements over the public address system added to the din.

Enormous banks of fluorescent tubes mounted high on the ceiling gave a greenish cast to the entire scene. This factory was a prime example of Britain's industrial might. The company had aggressively marketed the Sealand as a light seaplane for use in remote areas, using even the name to stress its versatile abilities on either land or sea. For a number of months, one company Sealand, christened *Festival of Britain,* was flown on a publicity tour of Northern Europe, the Caribbean and the United States. But sales in those postwar years were slow. Ours was the last one of the line.

Although the term "test pilot" implies the constant challenging of the outermost limits of human and aircraft endurance, most of the work of test pilots who work for airplane manufacturers is more mundane. These pilots fly each plane to make sure it performs well.

Whenever a purchasing pilot is introduced to a new type of aircraft, an experienced pilot in that model goes along on a flight or two to help acquaint the newcomer with the plane's systems, controls and flying characteristics. Such a pilot was assigned to check me out in a factory Sealand, since the one ordered by The Christian and Missionary Alliance was not yet completed. October 2, 1953 was the day I had my first ride in a Sealand.

Checkout was straightforward as far as the flying was concerned. This one handled very smoothly. But water landings and takeoffs on the choppy bay were another story! After a few of both with the check pilot sitting beside me, he said, "Now, go out by yourself and make some circuits and bumps." Perhaps, since he had no controls in the plane, he decided that if I got into trouble he wanted to be out of there before anything serious happened!

I made my circuits and bumps—especially the bumps in that choppy water—and returned to the dock. Over the next few days, I flew the plane several more hours, including fourteen night landings. Al, who had flown the Mission's previous Sealand in Borneo, did not need the same familiarization or the practice.

After several weeks, the new Sealand was officially turned over to The Christian and Missionary Alliance. The dedication was held on November 13. Dr. Bernard S. King, then treasurer of the Alliance, was there.

"Under the blessing of God," he said, "it is reasonable to expect that missionary history will be made by the Sealand plane, *The Gospel Messenger*." He went on to explain that the purchase of the Sealand had been made possible through the sacrificial giving of Christians in the United

States and Canada, and was intended not for personal pleasure, ordinary business or military purposes, but for the glorious work of bringing the gospel to tribes lost without Christ.

Representatives of the media, including *TIME* magazine and the British Broadcasting Company, were on hand to record the ceremony. As a tribute to the work for which the plane was intended, the officials of the plant circulated a notice that time would be granted for all employees who wanted to witness the dedication. Hundreds of them, bundled in heavy coats, formed a large crowd on the windy ramp.

Years of praying and planning and giving had culminated in these few moments under the leaden Belfast sky. Shivering a little in the cold, I joyfully recalled that in a few weeks we would be back in the tropics with our families and in the thick of the work. I did not realize then what a long and trying journey it would turn out to be.

The next day, Al went to London to get our visas renewed and to arrange with BOAC (now British Airways) for the hangar and servicing arrangements that would be needed along our route home. When the Sealand paperwork was complete and the checks had been run by the factory pilot, I flew the plane to London where we had what turned out to be a lengthy layover while more radio equipment was installed.

The following weeks were filled with numerous delays and frustrations. The installers worked slowly and encountered many problems. Then foggy weather closed in for seven days. We checked out of our hotel at least five times, only to return later in the day. We also spent many hours in prayer, searching our hearts, asking for God's guidance and His good timing. We were aware that even when we were able to get underway, Satan would try his utmost to subvert the Sealand's mission.

On Sunday, December 13, after breakfast, Al went to the room to pray, and I went to the little Methodist church next door. While there, God seemed to say to me that my service with the plane could require the supreme sacrifice, that being a pilot could cost me my life. It was as if He wanted a response to that idea.

I told Him that I was ready to be in His service regardless of the cost. I asked that first He would allow me a reunion with my family so that I could explain this to them. After much prayer and searching my heart, I finally came to realize that what God really wanted was my continual trust in Him to deliver, protect and lead as He would see fit, that *His* name would be glorified, not mine.

Finally, at 11 a.m. on a foggy, rainy December 14, we left London for Bordeaux, France. The weather was marginal. About 2,000 feet above sea level, we topped the fog and low stratus clouds. Since we could not see the ground en route, we were under what pilots refer to as "instrument conditions." Thankfully, just before we arrived in Bordeaux, the weather cleared. Hoping to refuel and head on to our next destination that same day, we were disappointed when the weather closed in. Later we discovered that, if we had not had a mechanic check our landing gear in Bordeaux, we no doubt would have had an accident in a few more landings. He discovered that the locking pin that secures the landing gear in the down position was damaged.

In addition, a paperwork issue surfaced. Without the proper clearances, we would be able to land only once in each country we flew over. Yet our flight plan called for a landing in Marseilles, France as well as Bordeaux. Officials explained that our only options were to land on the island of Sardinia, off the coast of Italy, or in Barcelona, Spain. This presented a problem, since our ground support group for fuel, lodging and clearances was BOAC. They would not be able to service us in these alternate destinations. After it became clear that new paperwork would actually be required to leave from any of the countries in which we would land, Al boarded a commercial airliner and returned to London to get our schedule in order.

To further complicate matters, the Short Brothers engineer and the replacement parts were delayed by bad weather, a strike of airline personnel and other complications. Each day we drove our rented car to the Bordeaux airport only to be disappointed by even further delays. Finally, on Christmas Eve, ten days after we arrived, the critical landing part arrived. The engineer installed it, then tested the plane. Everything checked out well.

We left Bordeaux on Christmas Day. At least one waiter in the hotel was glad to see us go. There, in the heart of France's wine country, Al and I had enjoyed the irony of ordering Coca-Cola every day with lunch, then sniffing the caps as a wine connoisseur would a cork. Sometimes, in jest, we lifted our glasses to examine the clarity of the Coke and to comment on its quality. The waiter was not amused.

Al made a good takeoff in heavy rain, and as we gained altitude the lower clouds became more scattered. En route, Al and I changed seats, and I continued flying to Nice, France, beautifully located on the French Riviera. As we approached the coastline, we again entered heavy rain. In addition, a strike of French air crews and communication personnel created a serious problem for us. Despite repeated radio calls from our plane to the control tower, we received no answer, no permission to land. Because of the heavy rain, I turned away from the coastline and let down over the Mediterranean Sea, leveling off at 1200 feet. Visibility was somewhat better at that altitude. We could now faintly make out the active runway at the airport.

The next fourteen of our eighteen flying days were not without peril, and we had many reasons to thank God for His protection over us and the plane.

On the Athens to Beirut leg of the journey, we were told to expect heavy cumulus clouds to heights of over 10,000 feet. I was flying first on this leg and continued my climbout to 9,500 feet. Soon the heavy clouds which had been forecast were visible.

As we entered these buildups, we promptly began icing up. Ice on an airplane is a much more serious matter than ice on a car's windshield. With a car, the driver can pull over and scrape the ice off for better visibility. But ice on an airplane affects every aspect of its ability to fly. Wings have a certain contour to them that allows the plane to fly. Ice forming on a wing can change its shape so the wing no longer lifts as it should. In addition, ice forming on any part of the aircraft weighs a great deal and can overload the airplane so it can no longer fly.

In a few seconds, our windshield was covered with a solid sheet of ice. The propeller spinners (the cone-shaped enclosures for the hub of a propeller) were covered with ice too, as were the leading edges of the wings. We had to get out of there quickly if we wanted to stay airborne.

In cases like this, a pilot will try to find either a cloud-free altitude with less moisture or descend to a lower altitude where the warmer air will melt the ice and prevent further formation. We opted for the higher cloud-free option and came out into clear air at 15,000 feet. No more ice formed, even though the temperature was minus 10° Celsius.

The next day, we were in Beirut, Lebanon, preparing for the next leg of the trip to Basrah, Iraq. For devotions that morning I read Luke 11. I did not realize at the time how much I would need to remind myself of two of those verses before the day was over.

Our main navigation instrument, called an Automatic Direction Finder (ADF), had malfunctioned on the leg from Athens and was impossible to repair in time for this flight. Since the forecast was for clear skies, we assumed that navigation would not be a great problem and that the uselessness of the ADF would not present an extreme difficulty. On the other hand, we had hundreds of miles of desert ahead of us. Oil pipelines could be used as navigational aids, but after departing Beirut, we discovered that those pipelines were obscured by a very low cloud cover. At one point, about 180 miles into the desert, the clouds thinned enough for us to see an important checkpoint.

However, another 120 miles into the desert, our left engine began cutting out and running "rough," as we say. Three hundred miles into the desert, with a low cloud layer obscuring the landmarks, an inoperative ADF and a malfunctioning engine was not a good situation to be in! With our heavy load of fuel, it was too far to go back *or* to go on.

One engine was not enough; we could not maintain altitude with this load. The lack of radio facilities in the desert meant we had to determine our position by time and speed. We knew that Baghdad was 200 miles to the north, so we charted a course toward it. I began calling the Baghdad airport on their radio frequency. They never answered.

Al worked diligently to keep the engine running by adjusting the fuel-air mixture, making delicate adjustments to the ignition system and just generally babying it along. We even gained a bit of altitude. Finally, a British Royal Air Force base at Habbaneya, Iraq, answered our call. They took bearings on our radio signal and told us the compass heading we should follow to fly directly to their base. Using their DME (Distance Measuring Equipment), they advised us when we were close enough to start letting down. We began our descent and broke clear at 3,800 feet, over a lake, with the runway directly ahead of us.

Once on the ground, we learned that this field had the only homing system in the whole Arabian peninsula and adjacent Iraq at the time! The Lord truly had prepared the way for us. How thankful we were for God's promise in Luke 11:9-10: "And I say unto you, Ask, and it shall be given you; seek, and ye shall find; knock, and it shall be opened unto you. For every one that asketh receiveth; and he that seeketh findeth; and to him that knocketh it shall be opened."

With new spark plugs on the left engine, we pressed on to . En route, we encountered very strong crosswinds, and, since we had no ground references, we were unable to check how far we were drifting. We were still eighty miles west of Basrah when darkness fell, flying on instruments, not by visual reference. At last, we saw a very faint beacon in the distance. As we got closer, we noticed it was a flashing green one. That was good news! A flashing green and white light is the international signal for an airport. We had found Basrah!

As we rolled toward the far end of the runway, we noticed a large number of jeeps following us. We stopped and shut down the engine. Dozens of fully armed soldiers dismounted from the jeeps and surrounded our plane. After they checked out our flight plan and passports, we were cleared to taxi back to the terminal area where our hotel was located.

Six days later, we arrived in Bangkok. Since the BOAC representative was not there when we arrived, going through customs and immigration proved difficult. Actually, in some ways we couldn't blame the officers. Since we had been flying into the sun for over a week, the glare through the windshield had made our faces red like tomatoes, leaving large white circles around our ears where the earphones had rested. We must have looked very odd to them!

They were also suspicious of a brand new British seaplane being flown by two civilian missionary pilots. No doubt our answer to the question, "What are you going to use that plane for in New Guinea?" tended to raise more questions than provide answers. "Taking the gospel to remote tribes who have never heard of Jesus and His love" was not the response they expected!

This delay was typical of others along the route. We had learned that it took time for official conversations, passport inspections and stamps, and the inspection of our cargo. Rushing through a foreign airport was not worth the risk of a few weeks in a prison! Finally, the BOAC field engineer in Bangkok came to our rescue and made arrangements for fuel and lodging. The next day, we left for Penang, Malaysia.

For many years, Penang, an island off the coast of the Malay peninsula, had been a luxurious base and resort for British military officials in the region. Later, in the '60s, when the Vietnam War threatened our missionary children's school at Dalat (Vietnam), Penang became the new home of the Dalat International School.

I was flying this leg to Penang. We encountered towering cumulus clouds most of the way. It looked like the bad weather would continue building that day, so after a quick meal and refueling, we were airborne once again and on the way to Singapore.

As we flew down the coast from Penang, we could see the dense jungles and high mountains of Sumatra to our right, but very little of our flight time that day involved mere sightseeing. With Al at the controls, we flew through one severe thunderstorm after another. Although we had bounced through previous bad weather on the way from Ireland, this leg was the roughest weather of all—gusty winds, dark cloud cover and heavy rain squalls. In some ways, of course, it was an appropriate "shake-down cruise" for the Sealand's subsequent service in New Guinea.

Malayan Airways officials met us beside the rain-slicked runway at Singapore. Soon the Sealand was safely sheltered in their hangar where white-suited mechanics conducted a scheduled inspection of the engines. Just as a new car needs an early inspection after a few thousand miles, a new airplane also needs careful mechanical attention in its early days. It was time for a thorough check of all the major engine parts. Al and I welcomed the two days that we would have in Singapore. We were both very tired and looking forward to a break.

We missed our families back home in Sentani. Today, we would have used e-mail or relatively inexpensive telephone calls to keep in touch, but in 1954 no such instant international communication was available. I still remember my thrill at receiving a telegram in Singapore from Elaine. It was the first contact I'd had with her since leaving Sentani fourteen weeks earlier.

5

History in the Making

During our layover in Singapore we took the time to reflect on how great God is. I praised Him for His goodness to us on our trip. Over so many miles and in such difficult conditions, He had been exceedingly gracious and merciful. We had never lacked, except in ourselves. I praised Him for my wife and children's health, and for His power to keep them during the ordinary, everyday life back in Sentani. Now, we were trusting Him for a time of refreshing and refilling.

One of the great challenges of answering God's missionary call is the separation from loved ones that this call often entails. Certainly we had known there would be the sacrifice of separation from our extended families in the homeland, but now we were also enduring a prolonged separation from our immediate families. Through all of this, we depended on God for His comfort and peace.

Several years earlier, Elaine and Ted and I had stayed in Singapore for two weeks en route to Indonesia. Now I had the opportunity to revisit places we had become familiar with then. The first place I visited was the great Robinson's department store where I made out a large food order to be shipped to New Guinea.

Walking the streets of Singapore brought back many memories: Bras Basa Road, Orchard Road, Orchard Place, Raffles Square and the post office. Down by the waterfront, Clifford Pier looked familiar; it was there that we had disembarked from a "lighter," the little boat that brought us from our freighter moored farther out in the channel of beautiful Singapore harbor.

On Thursday, January 7, we filed an instrument clearance for Kuching. This clearance would give us official permission to fly through difficult weather. Both Al and I were instrument rated; that is, we had special training and licensing certifying us as pilots who could fly safely under instrument conditions, once known as "blind flying." The Sealand was well equipped for such precision flight; some of the radios installed in London elevated our instrumentation to "state-of-the-art" of that time.

Kuching is located in territory on the island of Borneo, then known as Sarawak, part of British North Borneo related to Malaya. In the '60s, after a number of insurgent struggles, Sarawak and parts of the Malayan peninsula united and became the country of Malaysia, independent of their former British master. Singapore, however, would achieve its own independence, a nation by itself on the tip of the Malay peninsula.

Our turnaround at Kuching took only forty minutes, an enviable time for Southeast Asia. Soon we were in the air again and climbing through heavy monsoon weather, with the same gusty winds, thick cloud cover and tumultuous thunderstorms we had experienced on our way to Singapore. We were glad to have been granted instrument clearance, since a visual clearance would have grounded us on a day like this one.

The next morning, I was once again at the controls as we left the hot muggy island of Labuan. We gained altitude rapidly, finally cruising in the cool air at 10,000 feet, high enough to clear any of the mountains on our route along the north coast of Borneo. Our destination was the small city of Zamboanga in southern Mindanao, the Philippines. Zamboanga was the site of a vigorous Alliance work centered on the Ebenezer Bible Institute, founded in 1928 at the tip of a narrow peninsula protruding into the Sulu Sea.

After several hours of flying through rather heavy clouds, we made our first visual checkpoint of this flight—the island of Jolo. We were exactly on course and could soon distinguish the hazy coast of Mindanao.

Al was flying as we touched down on Zamboanga's gravel runway. Since we had cabled ahead to the Alliance missionaries, they were at the airport to meet us. We planned to depart from Zamboanga the next morning, so we serviced the plane after we had lunch with the missionaries. That night, we spoke to the students and had a wonderful time of fellowship. Excited about the arrival of the plane and the historical significance of the moment, some of the Bible school students hired buses to take them to the airport for our departure. The air was filled with singing as they held a praise service on the strip.

Such encouragement was timely, for within moments, some Filipino officials came out and "asked" us to come into the airport to speak with them. We followed, all the while trying to think of any reason why there could be a problem. The revelation which followed was most disturbing. The Philippine Civil Aviation Authority, they said, had received instructions from the central government in Manila to impound our plane, because, they claimed, the Department of Foreign Affairs had not been notified of our intention to land in the Philippines.

More red tape! We did have a valid clearance through officials in Singapore to make the flight, so Al sent a cable to the Department of Foreign Affairs in Manila to have the embargo lifted. With that unexpected delay, there was nothing to do but return to the Ebenezer Bible Institute and pray that God would undertake in the matter.

Early the next morning, we went into town and sent cablegrams to Elaine and Mary telling them of our delayed departure. However, as we reflected on the delay, we realized that God knew our needs and that He may have been giving us an extra few days of rest before getting home and back to work.

A message was waiting for us when we returned from sending the cablegrams. The Department of Foreign Affairs had approved our departure. We could leave when we were ready. We all praised God for this answer to prayer.

The next day, many of the missionaries accompanied us to the airport, prayed with us and bade us good-bye. Finally settling into the cockpit, we adjusted our seat belts and shoulder harnesses and began our takeoff checklist. As the sky in front of us turned a brilliant pink, Al pushed the throttles forward, and we set our course out over the Celebes Sea toward New Guinea—and home!

About 380 miles from Zamboanga, we traded seats. Since this was a very long flight, it was necessary to refuel in the air. Al crouched and crawled his way back into the cabin to begin the intricate operation. As he left the cockpit, I shut down all electrical systems. For these few moments we would be out of radio contact. Even some of our flight instruments were deactivated.

We had brought seven metal jerry cans with us, each containing five gallons of high octane aviation fuel. To replenish the fuel tanks in the hull, Al removed a small cover from one of the connecting hull tanks, unscrewed the fuel cap and poured the gasoline into a small hole in the tank. This, of course, was a very risky operation. Pouring raw gasoline in a closed cabin was dangerous, but it had to be done. It was supremely important not to spill any fuel. When the electrical systems came back on, the smallest spark could ignite any fumes which might be in the cabin.

The extra gas gave us another hour of flying time. This was a reserve that we would ultimately find we didn't need, but it was part of our strategy to make this and other flights as safe as possible.

Our 900-mile flight from Zamboanga to Sorong was the longest leg of our entire trip. In fact, we set a world record for distance in that type of aircraft. And, best of all, we were back in New Guinea—with the Sealand! It was an exhilarating feeling.

We refueled, then continued on to Biak, arriving there as night fell. We had flown 1,200 miles in a single day! In the hotel a little later, I could hardly keep my eyes open as I made my last entry in my journal. I praised God for the safe flight. It had been our biggest day, with the greatest distance flown and the greatest number of hours in the air. We slept well.

The next morning, January 12, 1954, we flew to Sentani. *The Gospel Messenger* was finally at its home base, and we were home with our loved ones. The plane went to work immediately. Within five days we were delivering supplies to the Wissel Lakes. But one of the main goals was to use the plane to open up the Baliem Valley to the gospel of Jesus Christ. Our praying and planning continued.

In 1938, sixteen years earlier, an American Museum of Natural History expedition, with wealthy Standard Oil heir Richard Archbold as its leader, had entered sections of the Baliem Valley to collect plant and animal specimens. Their plane had been landed on another fairly straight stretch of the Baliem River just south of our target site. They had made contact with the Dani people, but no members of their expedition were anthropologists or linguists, so they had collected little cultural information readily useful to a group of missionaries trying to contact these Stone-Age people.

Then, during World War II, when American military personnel were based at Sentani after the occupying Japanese were driven out (April 1944), weekend sightseeing flights were sometimes made over the interior. Douglas DC-3 transports, known to the military as C-47s, were used to fly groups on two- or three-hour excursions, the highlight of which was often a few minutes flying low over the gardens and villages of the Baliem Valley.

In May, 1945, one edge of the valley had been the scene of a C-47 crash in the mountain pass, and the later dramatic glider rescue of two soldiers and the WAC who were the only survivors among the twenty-four people on board. Those three people had been rescued from an area just twenty-five miles from our contact point. But, because of territorial divisions and fighting alliances in the valley, those few miles were like hundreds of miles elsewhere. Each alliance had definite boundaries, separated from other groups by an area of "no man's land."

About five weeks after the Sealand's arrival in New Guinea, we made our first flight over the Baliem Valley. It was a survey flight to check the river for future landing sites and get a general overview of the area. Bernard King, treasurer of the Alliance, Al Lewis, Einar Mickelson and two Dutch government officials were on board.

As we left Sentani, the weather gradually worsened. It felt like Satan was dropping a huge curtain to prevent us from entering one of his last strongholds. As we approached the high mountains, the rain and clouds were such that we were obliged to return to home base. However, as I began to turn the plane toward home, I spied a hole in the cloud layer over the pass leading into the valley. B.S. King wrote later about his experience of this flight:

> I still remember the white knuckles of the Dutch New Guinea Director of Aviation. . . . As we flew the length of the valley, I watched Einar [Mickelson] diligently looking at the various features of the valley. It was his first time to see the valley

> he had studied for so long. And, let us not forget, it was his knowledge of the tribal people that enabled the Alliance to have something you might call "first rights" there. That privilege was granted by Dr. J.V. de Bruyn, the local resident authority with political rights similar to that of a governor.

This was my first time to see the houses and gardens of these people who had been lost to the world for so many centuries. We were just a few hundred feet above them with the message that would change their lives! Giving thanks to God, we dropped low over the valley floor and followed the river downstream. There, we discovered a good spot that we would use as our landing zone when we returned in April.

Myron Bromley, who had been appointed to language analysis in the Baliem Valley, was in Sentani the morning of April 20. He had watched as the Sealand took off, headed for our first landing on the Baliem.

> The mission needed someone to work on the vernacular language. After hesitating because I was a bachelor, they appointed me to serve in what was then Dutch New Guinea, for probable ministry in language analysis in the Baliem Valley area. By that time, Ed and Elaine and the Lewises were moving to Sentani, and

> Al and Ed went to England to ferry back the new Sealand amphibian plane.
>
> In December, 1953, I went back to Meadville and spent some busy weeks packing to go to the field. Elaine's mother, with a taste for nice things, bought some Canadian china . . . and asked me to include the box with my outfit. Travel for both me and the outfit was by sea. After a late January departure from New York, I did not arrive in Dutch New Guinea until March 12.
>
> The first Baliem flights had been scheduled for March 24, but Mr. Mickelson, leader of our missionary team, became ill and was hospitalized. When he recovered about a month later, he set the date for the first flight into the Baliem for April 20, 1954, a Tuesday.

Elaine will never forget that day:

> The day of the first landing in the Baliem was a day of excitement almost too intense to endure. Sharing a set of earphones, Mary Lewis and I listened as Al radioed reports of the flight's progress. At last we heard his triumphant "hallelujah," as the plane landed on the river. The next thirty to forty-five minutes were interminable!

On the river, we were too busy to think much about how long this was taking. Because we had beached the plane nose first toward the bank, we could not unload through the large door on the left side. Therefore, all personnel and supplies had to go through the cockpit and out one of the side windows. This made the process much slower and more tedious than it would routinely be.

As we unloaded, our eyes scanned the bushes and trees just inland from the river's bank. We saw no one. Finally, what began as a small pile under a tree had grown to a massive load neatly stacked.

At last, with our passengers and their supplies unloaded, Al and I taxied up river for the takeoff. The landing stretch was much too short for a getaway, so we followed the river around a 30° turn and continued as far as possible to the rapids. The plane was now empty except for the two pilots. We had used up extra fuel en route and on the river, so there should be no trouble with weight for the takeoff.

With one propeller in reverse, and one in forward pitch, we pivoted and headed downstream. In the early '50s, being able to reverse the pitch of the propellers was new to smaller aircraft. Combining the propeller capabilities with our Rolls Royce "Gipsy Queen" engines, each delivering as much as 340 horsepower, meant that we had one of the most modern and dependable power plants available.

Elaine recalls, "Then, at last we heard the radioed report of the successful takeoff. Mary and

I were half-crying, half-laughing, but wholly rejoicing and praising God."

Myron Bromley was waiting for us at the strip when the Sealand returned:

> That evening, we all listened intently for any communication from the valley. Finally, we picked up the signal from the transceiver left with the party in the . "Sentani, Shangri La," came the call from the beachhead, using the name adopted for the Baliem Valley by an American army rescue party in 1945. Our Baliem party reported they were safe, but despite some hours of cutting a trail through the riverside underbrush, they had made no contact with local people. They had set up camp by the rising river, and needed to cross to higher land on the other side.

Myron would be on board the Sealand for its flight into the Baliem the next morning.

6

Dani Hugs and Tears

The day after that historic first landing on the Baliem, we awakened to a very clear morning. The afternoon before, Al and I had anxiously awaited word from the men in the Baliem at the 4 o'clock "sked," our abbreviation for a scheduled radio contact. Having a regular sked made it easier to monitor radio conversations from the Baliem, and they knew when we would be listening for their calls.

The missionaries reported that they had not seen any Dani tribespeople and that they were busy settling in to a campsite. We explained the weather situation that had prevented our second flight for that day, and said we hoped to make an early flight the next morning.

Myron Bromley, a Kapauku and a Christian worker from the north coast named Adrian were scheduled to accompany Al and me on this flight. As we lifted the plane off the runway, we were blessed with unusually sharp visibility. There were no clouds in sight! Below us, the dense green jungle, unmarred by the usual patches of low clouds, sparkled against the deep blue sky—another rare sight in the humid tropics. This was indeed an exceptional day.

Soon after takeoff from Sentani, we got our first glimpse of the mountains near the Baliem, their hard edges silhouetted against the lighter blues and grays of still more remote mountain ranges. We savored the sight, knowing that few days would be as cloud-free as this one.

In one hour and five minutes we were over the mountain pass leading into the Baliem Valley. As we looked to the right, we noticed another low spot in the mountains surrounding the Baliem, a pass paralleling the one we were now over. It was Archbold Pass (later known as Bokondini Pass or North Baliem Pass). Near it, and shimmering in the morning sunlight, was Archbold Lake, also named for the explorer. During his expeditions, Richard Archbold and another pilot, Russ Rogers, had landed their seaplane on that small lake to resupply a military support convoy that was exploring a land route to be used for evacuation in the event of an emergency. We had named the particular pass that we were using Mission Pass.

As we approached the valley, we noticed a nearly solid covering of clouds hanging low over it. How different weather could be in neighboring areas of our island!

After a legendarily clear morning at Sentani and en route, we were now confronted with thick clouds as we approached our second Baliem landing. We worked our way carefully through the layers and flew down the valley just a few hundred feet above the ground toward the landing site. We made a low pass over the river and could see the party standing in the clearing they had cut at the river's edge.

Within minutes, we were on the river. Since branches the missionaries had cut in the clearing work had been left too close to the edge of the bank, we could not get near enough to keep the plane out of the strong current. To stabilize it, we threw a rope to the men on shore. They would have to hold it tightly in order to steady the plane while Al and I unloaded it. Myron, "detail man" that he was, was attentive to many things neither Al nor I would ever see:

> The hour-and-twenty-minute flight, with Al and Ed at the controls, brought us over the riverside campsite and the little party waving up at us. A glance at the hill just across the river made it clear that the lack of contact with local people was not because they did not know about the newcomers. The hilltop was lined with warriors with spears erect, like one long picket fence, watching every movement of the plane. We landed. Al unloaded and inflated the raft, and we got out to join the party on the bank.

We learned later that just before the plane's arrival, the Dani had begun lining the hilltop and watching the strangers in their little camp in the swampy area beside the river. When we had called in earlier for weather reports, the missionaries had not yet seen the warriors and their spears.

During the previous night, Al had become concerned about the party's position in this swamp area and prayed that somehow we would be able to deliver them a rubber dinghy. That morning the Dutch Navy Catalina plane made an unusual early flight to Sentani, landing just as we were approaching the hangar with our load for the flight.

Within a few minutes of conversation, Al contacted the captain of the Catalina, and the navy consented to let us have one of the two dinghies they had on board. They also told us that it was unusual that they were carrying two, and had they been carrying only one, they would not have been able to let us have one. We took this to be a direct answer to prayer.

As we unloaded the dinghy in the Baliem, we told the missionaries how it came to pass that we had it with us. They too rejoiced at this obvious answer to prayer even before we called. With the dinghy, it would now be possible to transport supplies across the river to higher ground. The other bank would also be the best side of the river for the plane because the creek that enters the Baliem River there offered a calm wide place to anchor out of the main river current. Ironically, the move also would bring the camp to the side of the river on which the hillside warriors had been seen.

After the supplies were unloaded, we prepared for takeoff. We backed into the river, and I pulled in the 100 feet of rope. I am sure that it was a thrill for those on the bank to witness the takeoff. It was certainly a thrill for us. Again we praised the Lord for His care over every aspect of this journey.

Back at our base at Sentani, I made a low circle over the Mission settlement to signal our families that all was well. Although Al and I were in the air just over two and a half hours, we both felt as if we had put in ten hours of hard labor. These early flights were demanding, momentous projects. We were also aware of spiritual opposition and labored diligently to do our jobs well.

The next day we checked over the plane and waited until the Baliem party had time to move to higher ground. Al and I loaded up about 1,000 pounds of supplies that had been prepared for this flight: more camping equipment, bags of rice and other food supplies. Four of the larger items were attached to parachutes; the remaining smaller ones were prepared for free drops.

The radio contact that afternoon brought exciting news from the team in the Baliem. They said that they had located higher ground for their camp and had crossed the river successfully using the rubber raft.

Then came the best news of all: they had met the Dani! This too was a direct answer to our prayers! After all these years of planning and praying and waiting on the Lord, Alliance missionaries had made their first contact with the people of the Baliem Valley!

Myron would later chronicle this history-making moment:

> Mr. Mike assessed the capacity of the raft and decided to keep our party, now eight persons, together and take only the most essential equipment with us as we moved to higher ground across the river. "No one will bother what we leave now—we cut a trail for hours yesterday and met nobody," he said. We slowly pulled the raft upriver along the bank, then poled it across the river and looked back to see the baggage surrounded by local people!
>
> Mr. Mike decided that we should go on across the river and that Lloyd and I should stay and put up the tents there while he and Elisa went back to meet the men on the other side. The weeping welcome they received, the shouted signal across the river from those men, then the friendly bear hugs from warriors on our side of the river bore witness to the way God had gone before us.

Al had chosen the landing site as the

> one spot on the Baliem where he was satisfied he could land the Sealand. Over the next three years we learned that God had chosen the site, the one place in Grand Valley where the return of outsiders was desired.

Other areas in the valley would not have been as welcoming. The expedition in the 1930's, when Dutch military patrols accompanied Archbold and other scientists, had not always left a good impression. In some areas that intrusion was resented, and people who resembled that expedition (white men wearing clothes and living in tents) would not be welcomed for many more years.

We learned later from the radio message that not only were the Dani men friendly, but all fifty-five of them helped the missionaries move the supplies to the new campsite. "They are very friendly," one of the missionaries said on the radio. "They have invited us to their villages!"

This was a victory for all of God's people who had the burden for the Dani upon their hearts. We were humbled to be part of His doings.

On Friday we made a drop flight. We decided not to land on the river since the party had told us the water level had gone down. We also had a distinguished passenger along for this flight, Dr. de Bruyn, about whom the book *Jungle Pimpernel* had been written. Vic, as he was known, was one of the best-informed men in the world about New Guinea. He had spent many years in the interior for the Dutch government, studying the native cultures and getting to know the country.

In *Jungle Pimpernel*, he related many of his trips through the interior and especially of time he spent at the opening up of the Wissel Lakes, establishing a government post there. The story of his World War II escape from the Japanese who occupied the Wissel Lakes and other parts of Dutch New Guinea is thrilling. Vic occupied the right seat in the cockpit while I did the flying.

We delayed our scheduled morning takeoff due to bad weather at Sentani and toward the Baliem. When we had radio contact with the Baliem at 8 a.m., their report of the weather in the valley encouraged us to leave at once. We were soon in the air and within fifteen minutes were flying in heavy rain between two layers of clouds. Not until we were about fifty miles from the mountains that surround the valley did the weather begin to clear.

We entered the valley, and I began to let down through a small opening to the valley floor. It was apparent that there had been a lot of rain in the valley during the night. The Dani gardens were flooded with muddy water, and the river was higher than we had seen it.

I reduced power, activated the flaps and descended to about 400 feet while Al and Vic climbed to the rear in preparation for the drops. During my left turn toward the general area of the new camp, I picked up their mirror signal and noticed the smoke from the fire they had set to help us see the wind direction. Smoke fires helped us judge when and where to release our drops.

At a specific point in the first run, I gave Al the signal for the drop. As soon as the parachute was clear of the plane, I started a left turn for the next run. We made four runs for the parachute drops, then prepared for the free drops, the lighter bundles of supplies and equipment we would simply toss out without parachutes.

Although dropping supplies spares some of the risks involved in a landing and takeoff, many safety factors still occupy a pilot during such operations. A good drop, low and slow and accurate enough so that few supplies are lost, requires a great deal of flying skill and is accompanied by the same safety concerns.

During the free drops, we flew within fifty feet of the ground. We had to be lower than for the parachute drops so that the supplies would hit the ground at a angle or glance instead of coming straight down with full force. On this lower run, we descended to just above the treetops. As soon as I gave Al and Vic the signal for the drop, I needed to make a sharp left bank and then pull up in order to clear a high grassy knoll immediately ahead. This called for extreme concentration.

One of the Kapauku men was stationed on the top of this knoll to watch for any packages that might miss the mark. Each time I made the drop run and came near the knoll, he threw himself flat on the ground! Who wouldn't do the same? We made six runs and then an extra one so that we could get a picture of the camp.

When Al and Vic returned to their seats in the front of the plane, they reported what had happened during the drops. The first chute had failed to open. The second chute had opened, but the package was not roped strongly enough, and some of it broke away when the chute opened. The third chute had opened and lowered its load within twenty feet of the camp. The fourth chute had a steel drum attached, loaded with supplies. Again the roping was not heavy enough. When the chute opened, the drum broke loose, fell 400 feet to the ground and burst open like a bomb. We were all sorry for this misfortune, but it emphasized the importance of strong roping. The free drops evidently were more successful.

That evening, when we made radio contact with the party in the Baliem, the missionaries reported that they were able to retrieve most of the supplies. Only a few tins of food were lost. They also reported that some of the Dani had helped them gather the supplies that had been scattered when the packages broke up in the air.

Myron described the scene from his perspective on the ground: "Some chutes didn't open as loads broke loose, and drums smashed to the ground, mixing ink with clothing, and different kinds of canned meats into a mingled smorgasbord. We had more than enough to eat!"

Although the river level for much of the year was sufficient to allow the plane to land, there were times when it was too shallow. During those months, the only supply line to the Baliem was the airdrops from the Sealand.

The site of the first temporary station created a challenge since it was small, with dense growth surrounding it. There was a small beach area along the river that was open enough to receive air drops, but we could not use the drum/parachute method there because of the size of the area and its proximity to the river.

Low-level drops can be tricky. The question was how we could protect supplies being dropped at over 150 miles an hour with no cushion on impact.

One answer to that question came in the form of steel oxygen tanks from wrecked World War II planes still lying around . They could be used to deliver fuel for generators and kerosene for lamps. These tanks held about nine gallons and had a small opening that was secured by a screw-in plug. We dropped them "free," that is, without any covering or parachute. They bounced, but remained intact.

We also developed a unique method for dropping food supplies using two burlap sacks. In one sack, we packed canned goods and unpackaged rice, etc., into a tightly wrapped package. This sack was then placed in a loosely fastened second sack. When they were dropped, they skipped along the ground. During these bounces, the inner burlap sack sometimes broke open. The outer sack captured the contents and, cushioned by the rice from the inner sack, protected the other foodstuffs from being destroyed.

Apparently, it was true—"necessity is the mother of invention." In New Guinea, it was especially true.

7

Cowboys and Indians

The next morning there was a very strong wind with gusts up to sixteen knots at Sentani. Although it was safe to take off from Sentani's wide runway in such conditions, it would not be safe to try to land on the narrow Baliem River if there was such wind there. But on the radio we learned that there was only a very light wind in the valley and that there was a build-up of cloud at the south end of the valley.

That was both good news and bad: it meant good landing conditions, but, with the buildups to the south, those conditions might not last very long. We left at once. It was my turn to fly. This would be my first Baliem River landing and takeoff.

Our load on this trip included more Kapauku helpers, their rice and all of their belongings. It was 7:45 when the plane started the takeoff run. Five minutes later, I turned to the heading for the Baliem. Visibility was good, and all went smoothly through Mission Pass.

Once in the Baliem, I began a southerly letdown toward the river and maneuvered down the valley, gradually edging toward the right side. Al had suggested that we do that in order to check the river and help us orient our position for the landing. We dropped low over the landing area. Everything looked fine.

On the next go around, I prepared for landing, and Al got out his movie camera. This time, he wanted to shoot the entire approach and landing. As we started down toward the river, I adjusted our approach slightly to the left in order to clear a tall tree hanging on the edge of the river at the narrowest point. Once we were past this, a slight turn to the right lined us up with the river. As on previous landings, it looked as though our wings were almost making contact with the trees that bordered the river.

We settled into the water, and I made a slight left hand turn designed to keep us in the center of the river. Our landing run stopped exactly at a point opposite the little river inlet where we planned to anchor.

While Al was in the nose hatch preparing the anchor, I put the propellers in reverse, backed down the river about seventy-five yards and edged into the inlet at the mouth of the stream. Al threw out the anchor. I reversed the props to make sure it would hold. But the river bottom turned out to be soft mud, so the anchor pulled free. We had to try again. Even though it was frustrating to repeat the whole procedure, it was something that had to be done.

By this time, Mr. Mike and Lloyd were in the rubber raft and dragging a rope out to us. The other end was securely fastened to a tree on the bank. They threw the rope. It fell short. I thrust the engines into reverse to edge our way closer to the raft. But the force of the prop blast tipped the raft. Lloyd dived into the river.

The muddy Baliem was very swift and very cold. Lloyd needed to get back to the dinghy quickly. Thankfully, he was a strong swimmer, and in just a few seconds he was back in the yellow rubber craft, soaking wet from head to toe, grinning from ear to ear. We finally managed to secure the plane, and I shut down the engines.

Not surprisingly, our Kapauku passengers were a little reluctant to disembark! Not only had they witnessed the raft almost tip over, but when they stepped into it, the rubber bottom shifted under their feet. However, with a little coercion and amidst nervous laughter, they were safely unloaded, and we were ready for the return flight.

Al cast off, and we backed out into the current. I taxied upriver to the takeoff position trying desperately to keep to the center of the river. Earlier, at the turnaround position, we had noticed a very strong crosscurrent. I had to use almost full power to get safely across.

Now it was time to turn around and face back down the river for the takeoff. On earlier flights, Al had turned to the left. This time, we tried a turn to the right. It didn't work well, and during takeoff I had to cut back on the left engine very severely so that the force from the right engine would bring us to the center of the river. Our speed increased as we approached the bend.

At the last moment, before becoming airborne, both Al and I saw a huge log in our path! It was big and shiny from long immersion in water. There was no time to contemplate what would happen if our aluminum hull, traveling at almost eighty miles an hour, hit it. I pulled back on the yoke to lift us out of the water. It wasn't soon enough to clear the log.

First we heard a dragging, bouncing sound, then felt a slight contact with the log. Still moving at takeoff speed, we finally got airborne. Al and I didn't look at each other until we were well up in the air and beginning our turn out of the valley. When we glanced at each other, our looks revealed our relief and thankfulness that God had delivered us. Later, in our inspection on the ground at Sentani, we found where the log had hit. Thank God, the damage was minimal and would not entail a major repair job. But it had been a close call.

Before today's flight, we had talked about trying a slightly different route home. We decided to go ahead and check things out at another pass. We headed north above the valley, and Al took over for the rest of the flight. The new pass was somewhat lower in altitude than Mission Pass—that was an advantage—but it was also farther away from our landing area on the

Baliem. We decided that we would keep it in mind as an alternate route should that become necessary anytime in the future.

Our logbook entries revealed the things we were learning about flying in New Guinea. For instance, the next time we taxied up the Baliem for takeoff, we would instinctively turn the plane to the left. And, of course, the more flying we did, the more that habit would be ingrained. Other matters, though, were ones for weighing and considering.

For instance, the choice of which pass to fly through would sometimes be a matter of preference, at other times a matter of necessity. Even the issue of using a pass to get to the Baliem was, to a certain extent, a matter of preference. If the sky were clear between the Baliem and Sentani, a pilot could approach the valley at as high an altitude as he wished, passing over the mountain ranges and not through them. Yet the matters of fuel economy and the longevity of the plane would suggest that it be flown as low as safely possible. Decisions. Decisions. That's what flying is all about.

Al Lewis and I were friends who enjoyed working together. We respected each other; I was impressed by his spiritual commitment. During the war, he had been an instructor for the Royal Canadian Air Force and quickly realized that these skills could be paired with his vision for missionary service. After the war, he left a successful contracting business in order to become a pilot in Borneo for the Alliance. His background in jungle flying was an inspiration to me.

I don't recall ever having a real argument with Al. Discussions, yes, but no arguments. When we flew together, we each respected the judgment of the other. In an airplane crew, it is important that someone is the pilot in command; any other pilots on board are subordinate to that one. When he was flying, and I was in the co-pilot seat (the Sealand had no controls on that side), I didn't overrule or second-guess his decisions. And when I was flying, he respected mine. Often, in fact, we would talk over the strategies to be used in a particular flight such as a go/no go decision in marginal weather or when to turn back to base if the weather began deteriorating. We always found each other's advice useful in making those crucial decisions.

During the weeks of our long and tiring flights to deliver the Sealand to New Guinea, Al and I had sometimes needed a little space, a break from each other after the intensity of a flight. So we took separate hotel rooms. It helped us both to relax and be ready for the next day of flying, customs and immigration paperwork, maintenance checks and disrupted eating schedules.

When Al was on a flight, I prayed for him. And often, just before a flight, we would pray together. I suppose one could sum up our relationship with these words: We loved and respected each other.

In the next few days, we heard that Lloyd and several of the Kapauku had encountered some Dani in another valley and had been detained almost forcibly. Several Dani took hold of Lloyd's arm and held it firmly.

Suddenly, one of the Kapauku who was with Lloyd picked up a stone and, appearing to aim it at the Dani, called out, "Boom! Boom!" Another of the Kapauku did the same. Within a few moments, the Dani became confused or scared enough that Lloyd was able to move away. Where the Kapauku learned "Boom! Boom!" is hard to say—perhaps from our son, Ted, who had played Cowboys and Indians with them at Sentani or perhaps from their experiences with Dutch policemen and their guns in the Wissel Lakes. What really mattered was that it had worked!

Since this was the first report of contact with a great number of Dani, and so soon after our arrival in the Baliem, we trusted that God would bring further contacts. Now, for the first time, God's servants were there to tell them the wonderful story of Christ's sacrifice for all mankind—even the Stone-Age inhabitants of Shangri-la. We continued our fervent prayers for the safety of Lloyd, Myron and Mr. Mike, and for the Kapauku workers with them. We all recognized that such an experience as the one Lloyd had was not to be taken lightly; even the simplest situation could quickly turn violent. Without much language to work with, motives on both sides could be easily misunderstood.

The next week, we made another flight into the Baliem. It was 8:40 a.m. when I gave the plane full power and we lifted above the clouds. Up there, the sun was shining, the sky blue. Below us, we could see the tiny shadow of the plane slicing through rainbow-colored rings on the white layer of cloud upon which we seemed to be floating.

Again in an exploring mood, at the pass I made a slight turn to the left and maneuvered into the main valley through a smaller one. It was in this smaller valley that we once again saw huge natural limestone bridges, their chalky forms fashioned over the centuries by subterranean rivers, rising abruptly out of the mossy green trees. Some of the limestone was streaked with color—purplish blue and a deep orange. These magnificent geologic features, several hundred feet high, were breathtaking in their size and beauty.

The main valley was still cloud-covered at the north end and only toward the southern end did the clouds appear to be breaking up. Picking the clear spots as best we could, I let down to the valley floor, just 300 feet below the base of the clouds.

Once again, I kept to the extreme right-hand side of the valley so that we could easily make the turn to approach the river landing. With the log incident still fresh in our minds, we decided to make a low pass over the river to check for any debris that might be there. There was none, so we lined up for the landing.

Al had the movie camera running as we slipped down through the trees and landed short enough that we could taxi to the tie-up spot, thus avoiding the backup maneuvers of the previous flight. This time, the missionary men had anchored a buoy in the river for us to tie up to. Constructed from a World War II oxygen tank salvaged from military wreckage at Sentani, it was painted bright red with the same paint used for the large red call letters JZ-PTA on the Sealand. We had brought it with us on an earlier flight—another component of our developing infrastructure and systems to ensure that our flying could be as safe and effective as possible.

Soon Lloyd and Mr. Mike were alongside in their dinghy ready to unload the supplies. Myron and the Kapauku helpers remained ashore to assist in pulling in the dinghy.

About twenty minutes after we landed, everything had been unloaded, so we backed from the buoy and taxied up river about 700 yards to our turnaround point. Once in place, I opened the throttles. The banks began to speed by like a green blur. As we approached the turn in the river, the plane felt almost airborne, and about three-fourths of the way around the turn we left the river. Several minutes later, Al took over and flew the rest of the way to Sentani. Another successful trip.

That night, the radio report from the Baliem announced glorious news. After we had left the Baliem that morning, Lloyd and a few Kapauku had trekked north and east of their base station.

Some time earlier, they had made friends with a certain chief. He offered to lend Lloyd about twelve warriors for protection on this trip to a beautiful side valley called Pugima.

That day, as they walked into a village, twelve to fifteen Dani immediately gathered about them. The group later swelled to about 250. Lloyd did some trading with the people, exchanging cowrie shells for bows and arrows, stone axes and long spears. They were even able to bargain for a pig at a cost of only three cowrie shells—about four American cents. Shells were highly valued by these people in their own exchange system for which money had no value. Of course, the excitement about this trip was about the friendly contact with so many Dani, not about the purchase of such inexpensive pork!

In the years to come, Pugima would become the site of one of our Mission's first stations and the beginnings of a strong Dani church with numerous congregations. These were days of new and exciting beginnings. I was grateful to be a part of it.

8

Of People and Planes

In 1887, Albert Benjamin Simpson singled out New Guinea as "an area of great spiritual need." However, another fifty years would pass before entering that island would receive serious consideration by The Christian and Missionary Alliance (see page 316ff, *To All Peoples*). Then in 1936, a significant event, wholly unrelated to missionary work—except perhaps in God's mind—would trigger a veritable invasion into the kingdoms of darkness.

In that year, a Dutch aviator named F.J. Wissel, working for a Dutch oil company, discovered a network of lakes while flying in support of an exploratory operation. These he named the Wissel Lakes. Within two years of that event, and with the support and encouragement by the Dutch government, Alliance missionaries C. Russell Deibler and Walter M. Post were assigned to trek into the interior of New

Guinea. Deibler reached the Wissel Lakes in January 1939, and later that year both men established a post at Enarotali, near the shores of Lake Paniai. Their wives joined them in 1940.

World War II had begun, and the entire missionary staff (now including Darlene Deibler and Viola Post) and associates from the Makassar Bible School, with Dyak helpers, were temporarily evacuated in 1940. However, the Posts were able to return in March 1941, and Einar Mickelson arrived in December of that year. The first conversions were in August 1942, and by the end of the year there were 1,000 Kapauku attending services in about six churches, and the work of taking the gospel to the Moni had begun as well.

But the Japanese were advancing in the area, and all the missionaries had to be evacuated by plane in May 1943. Einar Mickelson, with associates from the Makassar Bible School, including two Kapauku believers, were able to return to the Lakes to resume work in 1946.

Then, in 1948, several other significant events occurred: 1) the Dutch government delegated Missions with the responsibility of educating local children; 2) the Alliance headquarters in New York directed the Mission to secure an import license for a plane and 3) the government gave permission for church work in the Moni and Damal areas.

> Though each event was important in its own way, the matter of an import license

> [for a plane] had special significance. It would spare the missionaries debilitating weeks on the trail, double or even triple their capacity for work, and enable them to launch one of the most dramatic and widely publicized exploits of missions in recent times. (*To All Peoples,* page 320)

Alliance missionaries had for years wanted to enter the Baliem Valley. In 1952, the Dutch government issued a permit to do so *if* a two-engine plane were used.

Those early ministries were expanded after the war and began to bear fruit. Kapauku Christians joined the missionaries in their expansion into new areas. The entrance into the Baliem was a prime example of this partnership. The Gobai family were Kapauku.

Although basic education and medical work were not a principal focus of the Alliance nor its missionaries, the offer of the Dutch government to subsidize school systems could not be ignored. The government also provided medicine, trained paramedical workers and subsidized the salaries of doctors in the region. All the supplies for this varied work were now transported by our plane. Let me chronicle some of our days.

It was Saturday. Today our job would be to assemble and pack a load of more than 1,000 pounds bound, not for the Baliem Valley, but for the Wissel Lakes. From the time the Sealand first arrived in New Guinea until our entry to the Baliem, we had made a number of supply flights to our missionaries at the Wissel Lakes. The flight would leave first thing Monday morning. Packing that many pounds was no small feat. It included 150 sheets of aluminum, two kegs of nails, sheets of glass and assorted-shaped packages of rice and other food supplies.

Monday morning arrived bright and clear. Al and I climbed into the plane and mentally prepared ourselves for a much longer flight than our recent ones to the Baliem. Again, our shadow looked like a small fly crossing an expansive and beautiful painting—God's painting. However, to our left, over the central range of mountains, were huge buildups of thunderclouds. The early morning sun cast an indescribably beautiful pallette of color on them—bright yellows, deep oranges, a rich reddish pink—with shadows and wrinkles many shades of blue and purple. It was strange that something as dangerous as a thunderstorm could be so beautiful! Through the breaks in the clouds, dark patches of jungle were visible, so dark they looked almost black.

After less than an hour's flying, we were over the broad valley of the Idenburg River that parallels New Guinea's great central mountain range. Flying over this vast valley, we made a mental note of possible river landing sites that might be useful in the future when the people of this area would be reached with the gospel.

Within just two hours after leaving Sentani, we were again in mountainous country. We knew from our charts and from previous flights that we were over mountains reaching 9,000 feet high. All we could see of them today was just an occasional glimpse of a peak laced with shredded clouds, a few quick glances at tumbling white-water streams, a brief view of jumbled rocks or a flash of tall, moss-garlanded trees. Soon we were ready to make a sharp left turn into the pass that led to the Lakes.

As we eased out of the turn and entered the pass, we were greeted with a rare sight. Still nearly thirty miles away, the lakes glistened in perfectly clear skies! It was a moment to be etched permanently in our minds.

We emerged from the pass and dipped over the northern edge of Paniai Lake, the largest of the Wissel Lakes. Al once again took out the movie camera, and we began our approach toward the mission station on the southern shore.

Since the lake is surrounded by mountains, the winds are often gusty and always uncertain. Today would be no different. As sometimes happens in mountain flying, we got caught in a mixture of air currents. Just as I touched the water, a powerful downdraft caught us, and we struck the surface at an awkward angle. The movie of the landing turned out to be a little scarier than Al had intended!

I taxied toward the shore and the buoy the missionaries provided for tie-up. The raft with the missionaries was already approaching the mooring station, and although we warned them to keep their distance, they continued to come.

Wanting to approach the buoy heading into the wind, I needed to make a circle behind it, but they did not know that. The raft was now very close and I was not able to maneuver properly into position. Al managed to hook the buoy, but our momentum snapped the rope attached to the hook. Unable to make another circle approach because the raft was now in the way, I threw the propellers into reverse, stuck my head out the cockpit window to see where we were going and backed gingerly toward the mooring station.

On his side of the plane, Al quickly took off his shoes and socks, opened both parts of the large window and perched on the sill.

When we reached the buoy, he gave me one last smile and lunged out of the window. With a resounding thud and splash, he landed directly on top of the pitching buoy and fastened the mooring line. Such athletic leaps were becoming a natural part of sharing flying duties with the Sealand! Fortunately, we both could swim and didn't mind getting wet at times, so the arrangement was quite satisfactory. Some pilots like flying seaplanes because if they get a little warm, they can always cool off during the tie-up procedures! Besides, it's fun to have a job that includes playing in the water!

We spent a few minutes of fellowship with our missionaries—Walter and Viola Post, Don and Alice Gibbons, Vonnie Heiden, Elze Stringer and Marion Doble. It might be easy for a reader to consider all of these flights as duties, as delivery assignments to be listed on a clipboard and checked off when completed. Someone reading about odd cargo loads being taken to strange-sounding places with foreign names might think of this as just some exotic version of a delivery route or of materials being distributed impersonally from a distant warehouse.

Instead, it is more accurate to think of our flights as being contacts between family members, the fellowship of God's people each engaged in an enterprise where the gifts of others were vital to the accomplishment of our individual and corporate tasks. The memory I have of the details of particular flights, of particular loading, of particular routes and changes in schedule, is due not to an interest in the mechanical recounting of details for details alone, but to the fact that, at the times of the flights, we knew we were engaged in vital support of our fellow-laborers.

What's more, it wasn't just the material support brought about by loading a cabin with food or building supplies or fuels for generators. No, often our arrival would be an occasion for sharing burdens, for group prayer, for warm conversations with and about family and friends.

Our visit with the missionary staff at Enarotali that day was typical of the hundreds of such meetings between pilots and missionaries to come in the following years as the ministries expanded. Unlike a mission field where transportation was contracted out to independent bush pilots or an existing airline, New Guinea was a place where missionaries correctly regarded pilots as part of the family, as brothers in the ministry.

Often a pilot would be met at the plane with a pitcher of cold lemonade and a plate of home-baked cookies. Sometimes we would walk the muddy path at Enarotali up to the missionaries' homes for coffee served hot off a wood-burning stove. Our conversation at such times would naturally turn to the struggles and difficulties we each might be facing and would often develop into a brief season of prayer.

Pilots, of course, tend to frequently check the weather, even during prayer meetings! A quick peek out a window at Enarotali, for instance, could show me if the clouds were building up in the pass to the north, if we were getting rain coming in from the west or if the wind was picking up on Paniai Lake. In an environment with so few flying aids and such extreme weather conditions, a few minutes could make a great difference in air safety.

On the other hand, a few minutes in prayer could significantly lighten our emotional and spiritual burdens and refresh us for the rest of the day to come. How heartwarming it was to be sent off on another flight, another hour of sweaty wrestling with cargo by a few words of prayer from brothers and sisters who loved us, who cared about our safety and looked forward to our next visit.

This day, at 11:15 a.m., we took off for Biak, one of a chain of coral islands at the mouth of what was once known by the Dutch as Geelvink Baai. Al was flying this leg, and Don Gibbons was with us to assist in getting more loads ready for the Lakes. In a little less than two hours, we once again landed safely at our destination.

9

Seaports, Airports

In the 1600s, an explorer named William Schouten charted a group of coral islands at the mouth of a huge bay on the north coast of New Guinea. In the years to come, the Schouten Islands became a hub for shipping and ultimately a Dutch military and airline center.

Mokmer, the town on Biak Island that is home to the airport, is laid out on a grid of streets, taxiways and concrete pads built by the U.S. Army in 1944 after a successful siege of the Japanese soldiers holed up in caves in the surrounding hills. Biak then was home to three airfields, all connected by a main road improbably called Michigan Avenue. It is not named that anymore, and all but the Mokmer airdrome were crumbling asphalt. Parts of those old runways, taxiways and hardstands were now the foundations of houses, shops and *pasars*, the crowded bustling marketplaces whose name is related to "bazaar." Like its cousin, the bazaar of the Middle East or India, the New Guinea *pasar* was a place of many languages, live produce, stinking dried fish, varied handcrafts, fresh fruit and sometimes raw sewage.

During the war, Biak was supplied by regular flights from San Diego (with fuel stops at Hawaii and an atoll in the Marshall Islands) in military C-54s, drab-painted cousins of the four-engined DC-4 airliner. The southeastern corner of the island is almost all paved, but now pocked with weeds and trees growing through the cracks. Until Australian dealers bought the last of them in the mid-'70s, the carcasses of scrapped airplanes abandoned after the war littered a large field.

Biak was also strong with the smells of the ocean, seaweed, diesel exhaust and the nearby jungle, whose limestone teeth burst from among dark vines and towering palms.

On the airport ramp, made of a light yellow crushed coral that shimmered blindingly in the midday heat, we serviced the Sealand and then checked in at the T'Rif (The Reef) Hotel, a simple wooden structure constructed by KLM, the Netherlands national airline, for its passengers and crews. The trees planted beside the building were not yet big enough to cast much shade.

Since 1929, only ten years after its founding, KLM, short for Koninklijke Luchtvaart Maatschappij, had linked the homeland with the Netherlands' overseas possessions, always using the latest aircraft available. Now, the airport at Biak was an essential refueling stop for KLM airliners, a stopping place between Manila in the Philippines and Sydney, Australia.

After dinner in the hotel's dining room, we went to our warehouse, a small, room-sized shed with a corrugated metal roof, rented from a local man. There, we prepared the load for Tuesday's flight to the Lakes (Wissel Lakes).

Tuesday's bad weather, however, grounded us. As always, canceling a flight because of bad weather was a disappointment, but we didn't let it became a frustration. New Guinea pilots get (almost) used to canceling flights because of bad weather. Besides, a day off gave us some time to catch up on letter writing, ordering more supplies, doing a bit of reading and a little shopping around town for hardware, parts and supplies that might be hard to find in Hollandia.

Given the pace of our usual workdays, a day when a flight was canceled was often a welcome break. Especially at Biak, there were usually interesting people to meet and converse with in the hotel lobby. Sometimes these were missionary families on their way to or from New Guinea.

The next morning, we were up before 5:30 so that we could get an early start on our proposed flights. It was very unusual to be able to make two flights in one day because the weather often closed the pass before noon. "Proposed" was definitely the operative word. This time, the Dutch surgeon on Biak went with us. An excellent photographer, he took along his movie camera to film scenes of Kapauku at the Lakes and incidentally to shoot a few scenes of the Sealand.

By 7 a.m. we were speeding down the runway with Al at the controls. On our way to the Lakes, we kept on the lookout for the KLM "Connie" that we knew should be approaching Biak from Sydney. Several times a week, a KLM Lockheed Constellation, painted with the blue and white Flying Dutchman logo, landed at Biak. Although the plane must have passed within ten miles of us, we failed to see it, probably because of the high clouds between us.

As we approached the pass to the Lakes, there were only a few clouds, and the scene ahead offered an excellent study in mountains with early morning shadows still holding onto the stillness of night. Often, pilots will circle a landing area to check the surface and get perspective on the angles at which a landing should be made. But this time, Al made a straight-in approach and landing. Within a few minutes, we were once again fastened to the buoy.

Karl Gobai, the native Kapauku pastor at Enarotali (not to be confused with Elisa Gobai in the Baliem), met us with the large raft. Fifteen minutes later, we were unloaded and on our way back to Biak. We left the doctor behind and told him we would pick him up on the return trip in the afternoon.

As we climbed up over the lake, we could see that the clouds were already beginning to fill in the pass. Because we had discharged our load and had some help with winds, we cut five minutes from the return trip.

When we arrived, Don Gibbons had another stock of supplies ready for us at the Biak warehouse. While Al serviced the plane, Don and I packed the second load. At 10:30 I signaled the tower and started the takeoff. Even as we climbed out of Biak, we could see the clouds accumulating in the distance. Nearing the pass, it was evident that we would have some difficulty locating the Lakes. The clouds had already filled in the valley between the mountains on the left (up to 11,300 feet) and on the right (up to 12,400 feet).

From our position over two small islands near the coast, I turned to a heading of 150°. This was the heading that would take us down the pass. I climbed a bit higher as we neared the pass and was now flying at 11,000 feet. Obviously, it is not good judgment to fly through clouds when there are mountains around you that are higher than you are! However, we kept going because there were numerous breaks in the clouds through which we could work our way without actually entering the clouds.

As we approached the narrower portion of the pass, I was able to run slightly to the right or left to miss some of the higher thunderheads and still stay in air clear enough to ensure that we would not hit a mountain. The wide part of the pass, perhaps twenty miles across, was at the northern edge of the range. Then, it narrowed, reaching its narrowest, about a mile wide, just before the Lakes. We continued down the pass for some time, and after about fifteen minutes were still unable to see the Lakes.

Finally, as our time was about to run out before we must return to Biak to ensure a safe reserve of fuel, Al and I saw a small hole in the cloud cover at the extreme east end of the lake. Below was the flat green valley on the east side of the lake. I slipped down through the hole and was on the water in a few minutes. This time we unloaded and set off again in just twenty minutes.

It was remarkable to see the complete reversal in the weather in such a short time. Now, less than an hour since we had been flying this route from Biak, the weather scene was totally changed. Where there had been clear skies, there were now huge thunderstorms. Before reaching Biak, we flew through a big black one.

After a few minutes of bouncing around, the magnetic compass swinging wildly, we burst out into clearer air. Soon, we were able to see Biak—under very clear skies. Once again, we managed to land safely.

But our work for the day had only begun. Since we always flew out of Biak in the early morning and were back before lunchtime, we chose to load the plane that afternoon. It is also prudent to service the plane right after a flight, so that it is ready to go on a moment's notice. We wouldn't want to put ourselves in the position of having to delay an emergency flight somewhere because we still needed to check the oil and fill the fuel tanks!

Since all items put on the plane had to be weighed and marked, we always had accurate counts of the total weight of the cargo. By the time we were finished that afternoon, we had handled over 5,000 pounds of supplies (counting loading and unloading) that day, and had flown five hours and twenty-five minutes. By 3:15 we were ready for our "midday" meal. It had been a good day. We were both ready for bed when the time came.

Our plan the next morning was to make an early trip to the Lakes and while there to have a meeting with Walter Post and Ken Troutman. At the time, Ken was field representative, the person in the New Guinea field of The Christian and Missionary Alliance who was responsible to headquarters for the personnel and business of the field. Al was flying as we took off at 7:10 a.m.

The weather was such a contrast to the previous day! It was so clear that we were able to see the mountains 130 miles away. Spectacular! They all looked too close because there was nothing to indicate their distance from us. The air was so clean that the clouds below us looked as though they would scrape the bottom of our plane although we were at least 1,500 feet above them. The Lakes were visible almost as soon as we entered the pass.

After the meeting, which concerned budget matters and policy about who could request use of the airplane, we prepared to return to Biak.

There were very few clouds in the pass this time. We could easily have made two trips had we known the weather would be so good. In fact, since we were finished with our Biak-to-Wissel Lakes runs for that week, and since the weather was so clear, I suggested that we return home to Sentani that afternoon instead of waiting until the next morning.

We had a number of spare parts for the airplane in storage at the navy warehouses on Biak. I called to have them brought over to us. In a few minutes, a Dutch Navy truck backed up to the Sealand's wide door and three sailors helped us load the plane and secure the cargo for flight. Several new tires, small aluminum parts in cardboard boxes, rolls of shiny aluminum control cables and a small bundle of copper tubing used as fuel line soon were on board.

Many other boxes contained specially shaped aluminum parts such as wing tips, a spare antenna mast like the one that protruded from the top of our cockpit, aluminum fairings that made the connections between wings and pontoon supports smooth, and even a spare pontoon, the rounded "outrigger" that hung from the wing to keep it from digging into the water. With such rugged flying conditions in New Guinea, we knew that the airplane would have its share of dents and scratches, and that sometimes bigger parts might get bent as well.

From his earlier Sealand experience in Borneo, Al had put together an inventory of spare parts that always kept us flying. Only once in New Guinea were we ever grounded because we were waiting for a part to arrive from Ireland.

As soon as the servicing was completed, we rushed to the hotel to get a bite to eat and gather our clothes. After a quick meal, we were back at the weather office making out our flight plan and checking out the latest information about conditions en route.

The operating manual for an aircraft gives instructions for the use of brakes, flaps and engine controls for special flight conditions such as maximum climb, short field landings and takeoffs, and various emergencies such as power failures and landing with a flat tire. Safe procedures for dealing with all of these contingencies had been tried out and documented by factory test pilots. When possible, pilots try to practice these procedures well before they are really needed.

As we were settling into the cockpit, Al asked me if I wanted to try a short-field takeoff. I agreed. We checked the manual and went through the motions. To our amazement, we were airborne in about 300 yards, even with our load of spares! The normal takeoff run is from 900 to 1,500 yards. By making this short-field takeoff, we now had some idea about what it would be like to use a jungle airstrip. In fact, while Al would soon be on a year's furlough, I was planning to take supplies to the Unevangelized Fields Mission (UFM) missionaries. If I did that, I would need to use their airstrip at Bokondini, which was only 700 yards long. This was good practice.

The weather continued to favor us. As we flew the sea route, we could see mountains of cumulus clouds, the tall, turbulent kind that accompany thunderstorms, to our right over the high interior mountain ranges. Although dangerous for flying, they were beautifully reflecting the golden hues of the late afternoon sun.

Organizing loads, planning flights, helping load and unload cargo—these were grueling tasks that were a part of our ministry in New Guinea. But sitting in an airplane cockpit with a spectacular view of a magnificent land in all its changing colors and varieties of cloud formations and lightning conditions was a part of our calling that often brought relief from stress and helped rejuvenate us for the next task at hand. The verses from Psalm 19 often came to mind: "The heavens declare the glory of God; and the firmament showeth his handiwork. Day unto day uttereth speech, and night unto night showeth knowledge" (19:1-2).

10

Troublesome Mags, Sputtering Engines

Back in Sentani after our series of supply flights to the Wissel Lakes, we again turned our attention to the missionaries in the Baliem. Eight more loads of supplies would be needed to fully establish that operation.

One Wednesday morning, the commander from the Dutch naval base at Biak was our passenger. Commander Aernout was going in to check for possible landing sites for the Navy's Consolidated PBY-5 Catalina. These large twin-engine patrol seaplanes had served the U.S. Navy well during the war and were now being used by the Dutch Navy to service its government posts. Commander Aernout had been very helpful to our Mission, most recently in authorizing the use of the rubber dinghy in the Baliem. We were glad to have him along.

Good relationships with government officials are always important to successful Mission endeavors. Einar Mickelson, the field representative of the Baliem area at the time, had worked hard and in a statesmanlike manner to establish a sound working relationship with Dutch officials. He had learned Dutch and studied toward his Ph.D. in Anthropology at Leiden University in the Netherlands.

Appropriately, all of our non-Mission passengers on the Sealand were attached to the government in some way. If the commander, a veteran pilot of the PBY's, decided a Catalina could safely operate on the Baliem River, then we would also have backup air support—from the Dutch Navy, no less—in case of emergencies.

We took off from Sentani at 7:30. Part of the time, the commander rode in the right front seat. It was a gorgeous day, and we were pleased with the good visibility. However, just as we were entering the pass, I felt the right engine sputter. Al and I looked at each other. Without a word, the commander gave up his front seat so that Al could more easily attend to checking the magnetos.

The ignition system on a piston-engined aircraft like the Sealand is regulated by a dual system of magnetos, known as "mags." These components, two for each engine, regulate the timing of electrical impulses used to fire the spark plugs in the right order. A problem with a magneto is often experienced as a drop in engine speed, measured in RPMs (revolutions per minute). An airplane engine can function with only the right or left mag operating, but of course, the best state over New Guinea's jungles and mountains is to have both mags working well!

When we checked the tachometer reading on the right engine, it indicated a considerable drop. Thankfully, the left was holding steady. I decided to continue into the valley, trusting that the condition would clear itself. We figured that this problem was caused by the spark plugs fouling with excess oil from the pistons, a situation that many times rectifies itself with further flying.

We entered the valley and I began my descent through clouds mixed with clear patches. The base of the clouds was about 600 feet as we leveled off. The commander took the right seat again so he could have a clear view out the front. I made one low pass over the river to check for debris. Out of the corner of my eye, I could see the commander turn and look at me. My eyes remained steady. I wasn't quite sure what he was thinking.

As I climbed back up, we went through the landing check, the usual list of procedures to be followed before attempting a landing. Then it was time to make the necessary steep turn onto the approach. Once again, out of the corner of my eye, I noticed the commander twist a bit in his seat. The closer we got to the river the more uneasy he became, especially when I slid down between the trees that bordered both sides of the river. I reduced power and nudged the control yoke back a tiny bit just as I felt the hull skim the water.

"So, do you think a Catalina could land here?" I asked, turning to the commander. All I got for an answer was a scowl!

It was good to see the fellows again. Einar and Lloyd and Myron all looked well fed and cheerful. It had been about two weeks since our last Baliem flight, and I had never seen them so healthy or in such good spirits. They were very grateful for the supplies and remarked several times about the quantity of cargo we had managed to fit on the plane. Besides the necessities of life, the supplies that would keep the operation going, our cargo often included mail and special treats for missionaries. Because of the air freight costs, fuel was used sparingly for cooking in the interior. So cakes, bread and other dishes were sometimes prepared in Sentani and sent in.

Since the commander was going to stay until our next flight, we decided to leave the plane tied up at its mooring spot on the river and visit the campsite named Minimo after the nearby creek. I was not prepared to see the camp as it was, so organized and clean! The large three-room tent, with canvas floor, was situated on a rise of ground with a small drainage ditch dug around the perimeter. Next to that was a walkway formed with small stones. Separated from the main tent was their cooking tent, and grouped together a bit beyond that were the tents for the Gobai family and the other Kapauku workers.

Around the whole campsite, they had begun to build a barbed-wire fence to help control the crowds of Dani who, in their curiosity, might easily overrun the little camp. In this area, and subsequently in other parts of the Baliem, especially at the Pyramid station, stealing sometimes caused problems that could lead to volatile situations. Diminishing the temptation with a fence was the method the missionaries chose to alleviate this potential problem.

While we were helping carry the supplies from the river's edge to the camp, we noticed a group of Dani men gathering on the opposite shore of the main river. Lloyd went after them in the dinghy and brought them across the river, and soon we were having our pictures taken with them. They impressed us as being very intelligent, as well as very friendly. This was the first contact with the Dani for Al and me, a very interesting one to be sure!

Only twenty-two days from our first landing in the Baliem Valley, here we were, two missionary pilots, greeting and trying to talk with warriors who prided themselves in their skill as killers! After praying so long for the gospel to penetrate this lost valley, and for the safety of our missionary brethren, we were greeting Dani face-to-face, our words translated by Myron Bromley.

When the time came for us to retreat from that Stone-Age valley, Lloyd gave me a dozen bamboo arrows and a bow, as well as a stone ax and a long spear. I'd asked him to try to buy me some to use as curios during my talks in churches on furlough and to decorate our home. Reluctantly, we trudged down the graveled path to the riverbank, climbed into the rubber dinghy and made our way back to the plane floating at its midstream mooring. With a final glance toward the small campsite, we expressed our gratitude to God for having learned firsthand that three missionaries and their Kapauku coworkers were comfortably established, making friends and beginning to learn the language.

It was Al's turn to make this takeoff. As he started up the engines, I cast off the rope, and we backed out into the current. On our way upstream toward our usual turnaround point, we noticed snags of tree limbs sticking out of the water. This made it impossible to continue, so we turned around much earlier than we usually did. Even as we made the turnaround, the current carried us almost seventy-five yards further downstream. Consequently, the space for our takeoff run was much shorter than usual.

Normally, we always had been near flying speed when it came time to make that 30° turn. But this time, with a shortened run, we would be traveling much slower as we approached the turn. With the airplane's hull still deep in the water and creating a lot of resistance as we went around the corner, we began to skip slightly to the outside of the turn. Al had to let up a bit, causing us to skim very close to the left bank. Finally, he managed to pull the plane off the water, and we made a steep turn, just missing the trees on the left bank. It was a safe takeoff, but we had been put into a tighter situation than we cared to be in.

I thought about the commander who was no doubt watching on the ground. I wouldn't have been surprised to learn that our takeoff had brought another scowl to his face!

The next morning, Thursday, we were once again in the air at 7:30 on our way to the Baliem. We had a bulky load aboard. Although the weight was the usual 1,000 to 1,200 pounds, this time it was cupboards and furniture that Lloyd had made especially for use in the Baliem, plus beds and mattresses.

Al was flying on the outward leg, and I was busy working the radio, giving position reports to Sentani radio and Biak control. Whenever an aircraft is in flight, someone keeps track of its position reports. This is called "flight following." Stressed even more in the years to come, by the 1980s the flight following radio conversations would be recorded on tape, so that if a plane were to be reported missing, searchers could replay tapes of the last position reports and not have to rely only on memory or someone's jotted notes. Of course, garbled transmissions or static could still be a problem.

On this day, we had unusually good conditions for radio transmission. Although Biak was

The *Gospel Messenger*, the Alliance's second Sealand amphibian, was one of seven aircraft the denomination owned during its years of flying first in Borneo, then in New Guinea (now Irian Jaya).

Bernard S. King, the treasurer of The Christian and Missionary Alliance, was a driving force behind those pioneer endeavors. He joined Al Lewis (left) and myself (right) for the dedication ceremonies of the Sealand at the Belfast, Ireland factory on November 13, 1953.

The first flight into the Baliem Valley took place on April 20, 1954. The plane performed well, taking off from our 3,400-foot perforated steelplate runway built by the military during World War II as an instant airstrip.

Elaine and our children, Ted and Lynne, along with Al's wife, Mary, watched with some trepidation as the Sealand disappeared into the clouds.

The Baliem Valley, discovered in 1938 by the explorer, Richard Archbold, was home to nearly 100,000 people. The Sealand made it possible to reach them with the gospel. Somewhere on the winding and tortuous Baliem River, we would have to find a place to safely land the amphibious plane.

The Baliem River, lined with tall casuarina trees, made an effective but challenging "runway" for the Sealand. Flying under such conditions demanded precise attention to safety practices. The Dutch Navy rubber raft (above) facilitated travel to the banks of the river. Here, Lloyd Van Stone (left), Al Lewis (third from left), Adrian (next to Al), a Kapauku Christian, and I (camera) came ashore with a small part of the load.

The windows and doors of the cockpit allowed us access to the equipment for fastening the plane to the buoy. However, it could be a tricky process.

The Sealand's large cargo area allowed for transportation of bulky building supplies like these. Reports by the Archbold expedition indicated a scarcity of timber in the Baliem, so early mission homes were prefabricated and flown in at great expense. Later, most missionaries built their houses with local materials.

Under the exchange program with Kroonduif, I flew large cargos in the De Havilland Beaver to our missionaries, including (L to R) Myron Bromley, Tom Bozeman and Ed Maxey seen here at Hetigima, our Mission's first airstrip.

The Baliem River was constantly changing. Heavy rains caused buildups of dangerous gravel and sand bars that changed the current. It was always a challenge to pick the right spot to set down.

Lake Paniai was a spacious body of water for seaplane operations. Here, Al prepares to take off for a flight to Biak.

The years in our little house on Mission Hill in Sentani were pleasant ones. The missionary community provided a place to renew physical, emotional and spiritual energies. Although each family had its own schedule, we knew we could count on each other to share in our joys and sorrows. Weekends allowed for some recreation at one of our favorite places—a swimming hole in an icy river running from Cyclops Mountain. And birthday parties, complete with homemade ice cream, always added to the fun.

Our Land Rover provided the means to make frequent trips to Hollandia to buy supplies of all kinds for our fellow workers in the interior. In fact, a large hangar near the Sentani airstrip allowed for storage and packing of materials ranging from fuel to food to furniture.

The old ways and new ways were in stark contrast on every airstrip that we served. At the Pyramid runway, 18-foot hardwood spears wielded by Dani warriors lend a backdrop for the Cessna that interrupted a local war.

The Homeyo airstrip was an engineering feat;
Moni workers dug clay that would be used as a surface for the runway.

Running on the airstrip was one way to help compact the new clay surface.

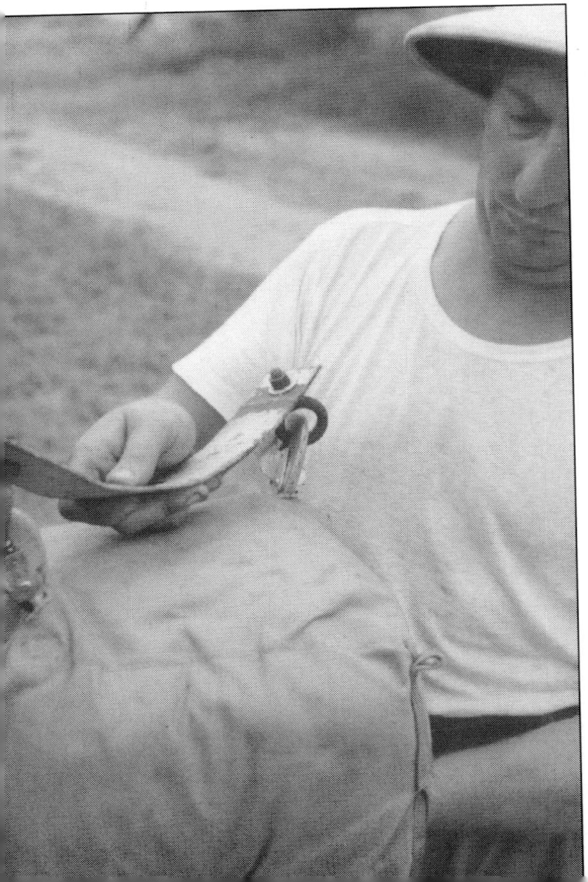

Dick Lenehan was a vital member of the Aviation Section. His mechanical skills and engineering capabilities kept our planes well maintained. He also designed a fastener to attach a parachute to a 55-gallon steel drum, thus permitting the dropping of heavy loads when the river was too low for a safe landing.

Even a kitten was safely airdropped to three-year-old Johnny Cutts as a Christmas gift.

Only the missionaries were concerned about this landing at Homeyo. The Mon had never seen a plane land before; they thought this was routine. Both wheel broke through the thin layer of clay covering, causing the plane to flip over.

Using a makeshift crane and block and tackle, we managed to lift the damaged plane onto its wheels. It was eventually flown to our hangar at Sentani for more permanent repairs.

Ken Troutman and Mr. Hamers, the civil aviation director, later inspected the undamaged portion of that airstrip. Behind them, a 1500-foot drop-off marks the end of the runway.

On November 3, 1956, a new Cessna was dedicated at the Obano airstrip (above). The next day, it was destroyed by Kapauku warriors, and an Indonesian Christian teacher and his family were killed. Cargo was stolen.

Gordon Larson and Don Gibbons worked far away from their families for months at a time so that the Ilaga station could be established.

Within several weeks, the civil aviation director inspected the strip and gave permission for Peggy Larson and children to enter the Ilaga. They were warmly welcomed by the people.

I lost track of the number of rattan bridges we crossed on our long journey to the Ilaga. The purpose of the trip was to inspect the newly constructed airstrip before we landed a plane on it. We did not want a repeat of the problem encountered earlier at Homeyo.

Communal meals were prepared by steaming potatoes in a grass-lined pit heated with rocks. Sometimes pork was cooked in the same pit. It was not hard to get a crowd later once the plane landed.

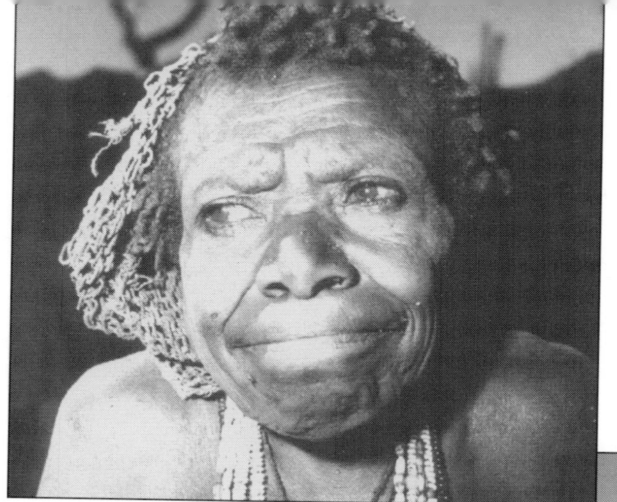

Faces.

Everywhere I flew in New Guinea, I was captivated by the people our missionaries were reaching with the gospel.

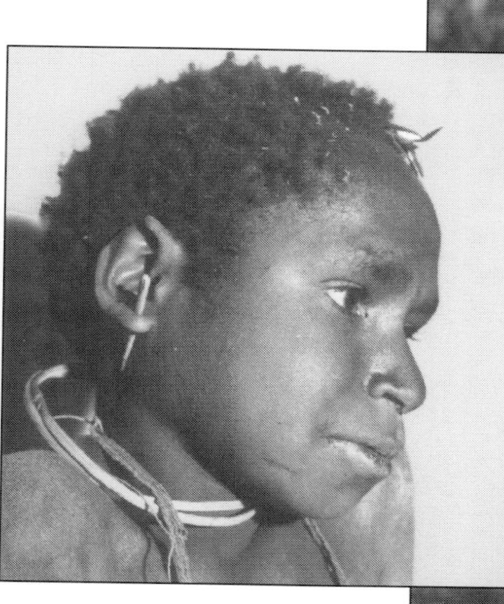

All of these were from the Baliem valley.

Al Lewis and I made numerous supply flights to Enarotali at the Wissel Lakes. One particular afternoon, Al and Mary joined us for a late afternoon walk on the hangar property near Lake Sentani and within sight of the hills where General MacArthur made his headquarters before reclaiming the Philippines.

In 1955, while Council was in progress at Philadelphia, Al crashed his plane into the side of a mountain. This stained glass window, in his memory, impresses visitors to the Alliance offices in Wassenaar, the Netherlands.

Although the Cessna 180 opened up new opportunities for the Mission and changed the way missionaries thought about aviation, in 1957, the Alliance turned over its operation to MAF. (L to R: the Van Stones, Mickelsons, Lenehans, myself and Ken Troutman.)

Subsequently, I was hired by Air America, a CIA operation, to be their chief pilot and deputy base manager in Southeast Asia. My duties included giving proficiency check rides with pilots (above), making crew schedules, liaison with "customers," overseeing maintenance, security and flying missions. I was permitted to assist our missionaries in any way possible as long as there was no actual cost to the airline.

In August 1999, Elaine and I celebrated our 50th wedding anniversary.
We are grateful for the many years God has given us to serve Him together.

over 300 miles away, we were able to talk to them as though we were using the telephone.

About ninety miles out of Sentani, the right engine began again to run rough. Al checked the mags. This time both showed a drop in RPMs. The trouble we had the previous day had been cleared up, so we could not help but feel concerned about today's repetition, especially when both mags indicated a drop in power.

We proceeded on toward the pass, trusting that again the condition would clear up, but instead the roughness began to come with increasing frequency.

"What do you think, Ed?" Al asked as we approached the pass.

"Well, I think it's up to you. You're the one doing the flying."

A pause.

"I think we better return to Sentani," he said finally.

I agreed.

As we turned toward home, we climbed as high as we thought necessary in case the engine failed completely. A light plane like the Sealand can glide a considerable distance even if both engines fail. This distance is measured in terms of "glide ratio." If a plane has a glide ratio of twelve to one, it can glide with engines turned off twelve miles horizontally for every mile of altitude. In addition, higher altitude would give a pilot more time to retry starting the engines and to report his problem and location.

Even though it is a little counter-intuitive, the pilot of an airplane in trouble tends to try to fly higher rather than lower. Of course, having more distance to glide also increases the number of areas one can try to choose to land. That, however, is usually a moot point in the jungles of New Guinea!

By this time, I had radioed Sentani and Biak that we were returning and told the Sentani tower to expect us in about one hour. About half way there, Al shut down the right engine and "feathered" the propeller, changing the pitch (angle) of the propeller blades to lower air resistance. An unfeathered propeller on a stopped engine can slow a plane down considerably. That wasn't something we wanted! At our altitude of 12,000 feet, and with the load we were carrying, we were losing about 200 feet every minute. The air is thinner the higher one flies and can't support as much load as the air lower down. We descended to 6,000 feet and were relieved to find that we could maintain our altitude on the power from only one engine.

We continued descending toward the airport at Sentani. As Al circled the field, he started the right engine again in order to give some thrust during our landing. It is possible to land a twin-engine airplane with only one engine running, but it is not an easy maneuver. In that situation, the plane is steeply "crabbed" as it makes the final approach to the runway, and the pilot has to straighten it out just as the wheels touch or something could break.

The right engine gave us the power we needed to make a smooth landing. Pilots are trained to be cool during emergencies, to work efficiently at minimizing problems and to keep thinking clearly. So we had little time to worry about the danger we were in. Certainly an engine failure and a crabbed landing were not the routine flying conditions we would have wished for, but our trust was in God.

We were back on the ground at 9:20, but we had a busy day ahead of us. We pulled the big engine work stand under the right engine and began to search for the trouble. First, we took out all of the plugs. Here we discovered some of the problem. On one side of the cylinder the spark plugs had fouled badly, their electrodes contaminated with oil. In some cases, the points of the plugs had welded across, meaning that they could produce no spark. We put a new set of spark plugs on one side of the engine and cleaned and reset the other set of plugs from the opposite side.

Next, we checked the magnetos. Both mags of the right engine had excess oil in them, and one mag had an incorrect point setting. So we corrected these problems, and about 1:30 we were ready to start the engine and run it for a while to see if we had gotten to the bottom of the problem. Al stood near the engine while I started it up so that he could watch the exhaust stacks for puffs of black smoke that would indicate burning oil, something we hoped had been corrected.

The first engine run showed a considerable drop in RPMs again. So it was off again with the engine cowling to check and fix the mags again. Finally, when we ran up the engines the second time, everything was satisfactory. By that time, it was late afternoon. We were glad to call it a day.

A day like that really made us feel the strain. Long hours, dangerous flights and the heavy burden of responsibility for supplying a huge mission field were all part of the physical, emotional and spiritual load we carried.

11

Boredom Punctuated by Sheer Terror

On Friday morning we were in the air by 7:15 on our way to the Baliem. The weather was not the best at Sentani, but as we cleared a few layers of cloud and reached a cruising altitude of 10,000 feet, we could see the mountains surrounding the valley. The pass itself appeared to be closed in by a solid layer of cloud. But, once in the valley proper, we noted some breaks at the far end and were able to let down in and out of cloud to the valley floor.

I made a pass over the river, then pulled up to an altitude suitable for a landing approach. Because trees had been cut from the banks of the narrowest portion of the river, we could now land at that point. This time we were able to stop in almost half the distance previously needed.

Once again, we were greeted by the men, and Al went ashore to take movies of the unloading of supplies. One hour later, we were ready to depart. Although Commander Aernout was to return with us to Sentani, he protested that this was much against his desire since he had greatly enjoyed his two days in "the land that time forgot." He also commented on our takeoff of the previous day and hoped sincerely that it would not look so close today! We decided it was best not to tell him that we had never taken off with three aboard before, as we would today, and that we would be taking off from the same place in the river as before!

The snags and big trees in the water with junk trailing from their branches were still there, blocking our usual turn-around point. I taxied upriver to the last possible foot and made the turn. Although we were not quite ready to take flight as we reached the sharp corner, about three quarters around it we became airborne. From there on everything went well.

Once through the pass, I traded places with the commander so he could do some flying. He was very impressed with the plane and the way it handled. The Sealand certainly was much smaller, lighter and more responsive than the powerful, heavy Catalina he usually flew. As we neared Sentani, I took over again and made the approach and landing while Al took movies. We were back on the ground by 10:40.

The next flight we made to the Baliem was June 5, three weeks later. During the intervening time, the missionaries in the Baliem made extensive checks on the river. They searched for areas where the current was slower, they measured the length of straight areas, and they removed snags, including the one that had plagued our last two flights. They also cleared even more trees from the banks at various places, giving us much clearer approaches.

Through radio contact with the Baliem, we learned that the river had dropped a total of twelve feet since our first landing in April. Because of this, a new plan for landing and takeoff had to be considered. Sandbars now dotted sections of the river that we had used previously. Earlier in the week, the men reported that the river had risen five feet. They suggested I try to get in as soon as possible. The first possible day was Saturday, but by then the river had dropped again.

I did a radio check with the Baliem at 7 a.m. and learned that the weather was favorable. So we took off promptly at 7:50. Dick Lenehan, our missionary engineer who had recently arrived in Sentani, came along—his first trip to the Baliem.

Dick was impressed with his first glimpses of the valley with its patterns of drainage ditches, the unusual brown grass-thatched houses and tall watchtowers. In some areas of the valley, the Dani had built wooden towers of saplings lashed together. The small platform on the top made it possible for a watchman to spot any enemy movement in the fields and woods beyond. If invaders were spotted, the watchman would yell for reinforcements and direct their movements toward the invaders.

We managed to slip down through the trees bordering the river and made a short landing. It was good to greet the men again. They looked well and happy. The Kapauku men had a few gifts for me—a foot-high headdress made with dog fur and a "duster" made from bird feathers, used by the Dani in battle and in their victory dances. Lloyd also gave me about thirty arrows, three bows and a stone ax. These had been bought with knives I had left there earlier for that purpose.

While we were unloading the plane, many Dani gathered along the bank of the river scarcely twenty feet away. This was the closest they had come while the plane was there. Many more waded and swam across the river toward us. One Dani in particular was determined to board the plane. Evidently he had caused some trouble in his village and had been beaten for it. Now he wanted to get away. It took some effort to stop him from entering the plane.

This Dani was unusually large. His strength soon made us realize we were at a disadvantage. For one thing, we were confined to the small opening of the cockpit and were not as agile as he was in his bare feet. We could easily have been pushed into the river. After several missionaries came to our assistance, he was overpowered.

We got back on board. After some trouble starting the right engine, we cast off and began taxiing. I decided to head upstream about 200 yards beyond where we had moored. That would give me a running start into the straight stretch. Cautiously I made a turnaround in half of the river and headed down with full power. I made the 30° turn by easing off on the throttle to that engine, then brought it up quickly to full power and headed down the straight section. The plane came off the water well, we cleared the trees and, with God's help, had an uneventful return trip except for a slight roughness in the right engine.

During those days when the water level was receding, we talked frequently about the future use of airstrips to supplement our water operations. Would it be possible to build strips in the interior? Who would do it, and how? These were busy and sometimes exhausting days. During times like this, prayer support from friends and family and church folks in the homeland became a lifeline just as vital to us as our physical supplies were to our fellow missionaries.

After the Baliem flying had ceased for the season, Elaine and I wrote a letter to our families and supporters, outlining some of the significant events in our lives and in the progress of the gospel in New Guinea:

> We all have been busy these past months, especially since the Lewises have returned to the States for their furlough.

> Dick and I have been flying supplies to the Wissel Lakes and the Baliem regularly and doing the usual ground work and office work.

Just two weeks before that letter, we had said good-bye to Ted, our son. We wanted him to be able to get a full school year in at home before he came back for another two-year term on the field (aviation people had shorter terms than other missionaries). Instead of having him wait to go on furlough with us and begin school late, we sent him on ahead. He was very excited about the trip. For an eleven-year-old to travel halfway around the world alone was not a common thing. Needless to say, we were relieved when we heard that he had arrived safely in Sharon, Pennsylvania.

The last landing that was made in the Baliem that season was on the twenty-sixth of June when Einar Mickelson was brought out to rejoin his family in the States. For the next few months, the river was so low that we were unable to make landings in the valley. We had known that it would drop after the rainy season but were not prepared for it to happen so soon.

We had been able to fly in necessary items for establishing a semi-permanent camp, but we had not been able to stockpile all of the supplies needed for the six-month dry period we knew was coming. For the next five months we prayed that Lloyd, Myron, the Gobai family and other Kapauku workers would have no emergency that necessitated anyone's coming out. It just wasn't possible.

Yet the missionaries in the Baliem did have emergencies. Unknowingly, they had located their new camp in a section of "no man's land." Frequent battles were fought between warring tribes right on their doorstep. And occasionally, a few Dani would appear around the camp, only to be ambushed and killed on the spot by their enemies.

During this period, we dealt with the supply problem by attaching fifty-five-gallon drums filled with supplies to large surplus cargo chutes and dropping them. We even dropped gasoline for running a small generator and kerosene for lamps. These fuels were "free dropped" in surplus oxygen bottles, each holding about nine gallons.

About this time, Jerry and Darlene Rose and their two sons returned to the field and were waiting eagerly to make their entry into the valley. However, the governor had made a ruling that no children would be permitted in the interior until the government established a post. We prayed, and the policy was changed. Even before the first government post was established at Wamena in 1956, entire Alliance missionary families were able to live in the Baliem.

Lloyd and Myron have had many opportunities to praise God for His faithfulness. During one very serious situation in which the missionary men were in the middle of a native battle, the Lord overruled and gave the men their first real contact with a village and a large number of people. These villagers were so insistent that the men move into their village that the men did divide their base camp and began taking turns living in the village. Within one week, the villagers had built them a native-type wooden house.

It was at this time that Lloyd revisited an area where the people previously had not been too friendly and refused him permission to enter their villages. This time, he found them still somewhat skeptical, but the Lord opened the way, and Lloyd was able to give an old Dani man a penicillin injection for a skin disease called yaws. Soon others gathered. After he had given many shots, Lloyd was invited to the local leader's home. He offered Lloyd bananas and other things and invited him to stay in their village.

Since it was toward late afternoon, Lloyd declined the offer. On the way back to the base camp, however, the old chief showed Lloyd an ideal spot for a camp. Perhaps this would be the Mission's next big move as soon as other personnel arrived in the valley. Eventually that spot became the Hetigima station, home to several missionary families and the site of a Dani Bible school.

At the same time, Myron had been doing well with the language. Effective language learning often depends on immersion in the culture. Myron took full advantage of the opportunities and spent a lot of time in Dani villages, often eating an evening meal of steamed sweet potatoes and greens with the people and then wending his way home with the aid of a flashlight. Some nights he chose to stay in the village, for he found that the smoky fires continuously burning in a Dani hut kept mosquitos and many other insects away. However, they did make breathing almost impossible!

The more the work progressed in New Guinea, the more we came to realize that we had other important duties aside from flying. During one week at the Wissel Lakes we met as an executive committee for about fifteen hours, seeking guidance regarding the future development of the field. These were days of seeking God's face and trusting Him to direct us in each new step. What the future held, we did not know. Only God knew. It was best that way.

During the season when the Baliem River was low, we caught up with the supply loads to the other areas. On one flight to the Wissel Lakes, we were accompanied by the Cutts family. From a village reached by boat from Enarotali, they would walk to their station at Homeyo, a journey of about three days. (See *"Weak Thing" in Moni Land* by William Cutts, Book 2 in The Jaffray Collection of Missionary Portraits.)

The Sealand had been prepared and loaded the night before, and we were all ready to take off. The weather at 7 a.m. was very cloudy, but we noticed that the layer of clouds was not very thick. Judging from experience, we predicted that it would burn off by noon. The weather report from Biak indicated that we could expect fair weather. So I decided to take off immediately and get the weather report for the Lakes after getting in the air.

Dick Lenehan, acting as copilot, checked our path over the ground. Bill Cutts was also surveying the ground below, but he was not trying to measure wind drift. Instead, he was occupied with trying to locate native houses. In those days, almost everywhere we flew in New Guinea was a pioneer route. Finding villages or clusters of thatched-roof houses from the air could help missionaries estimate population in these unexplored areas. In fact, some of the last people groups to be reached on the island of New Guinea would be found on the route from Sentani to the Wissel Lakes.

Today, we had a good tailwind, and in just a little over two hours were ready to turn into the pass to the Lakes. The landmark we used for this turn was a 9,600-foot mountain, with a rather distinctive conical shape. It soon became known to pilots as Mt. Ulrich. I always enjoyed hearing the tower crew at Sentani or Biak acknowledge my position report on this route with a merry "Roger, over your own mountain!"

Over the Lakes, we saw that Ken Troutman had come out on the raft to meet us. After discharging the Cutts family and taking Harold Catto on board, we were ready to depart for Biak. Harold was going to the warehouse there to help get loads ready for the remaining three trips. Once again, the right engine began to run rough. At Biak, Dick changed the points and installed a new set of plugs.

The next morning, Dick and I took off for the Lakes at 7:50 a.m. After landing on Lake Paniai, we loaded the Cattos' refrigerator and other baggage, and Ken Troutman and I took off for a ten-minute flight to Lake Tigi, just over a ridge. Since Ken had become board representative, his family had moved to Lake Paniai, and the Cattos had gone to Tigi. We unloaded the refrigerator and other household items at Tigi, then loaded on a few of the Troutmans' belongings for the return trip to Lake Paniai.

The weather the next morning was poor. There had been considerable buildup during the night, and the forecast was for continued activity. But after hearing a radio report from the Lakes, we decided to go. The weather en route was not good, but it was good enough to be able to see the tops of the mountains on either side of the pass. That was really all that was necessary.

We let down at the Lakes and made a landing toward the dock. Bill and Ken met us with the raft, and we all returned to shore. Ken had called an executive committee meeting. After the meeting, we returned to deteriorating weather in Biak.

Dick serviced the plane while I contacted the Navy to get another load of spare parts. After a quick lunch at the hotel, we took off for Sentani and home. It had been a long day—about six hours of actual flying plus loading and unloading thousands of pounds: furniture, appliances, supplies—and people.

Perhaps these accounts of long hours, tedious flights, mundane loads flown from point A to point B, then another load flown from point B back to A may seem pointless and boring. One professional pilot described his job as "long hours of boredom punctuated by minutes of sheer terror!" Yet for Christian pilots, supplying pioneer missionaries in one of the world's last true frontiers, our work was vital. We were very aware of the great importance of our work in facilitating the spread of the gospel to every tribe, tongue and nation.

Many times, during flight, we would pray specifically for the missionaries who would receive the medicine to treat illnesses that had run rampant in those parts for perhaps centuries. Yaws, a skin disease, was one of the worst. It could grotesquely disfigure a person in relatively few years. When missionaries first entered the interior of New Guinea, they counted hundreds of cases, many of which ultimately resulted in death. Yet one penicillin shot could begin the healing process. Yaws is now almost unknown in these areas.

We also prayed for the thousands of children, yet unborn, who would hear the gospel in the schools and churches that would be built with the lumber, the roofing aluminum, the hardware we carried on board.

Although conversation was not easy in an airplane like the Sealand because of the engine noise and the separate passenger compartment, the passengers we carried were often friends. These friendships developed over numerous conversations on docks, on runways, in warehouses and as together we shouldered heavy loads. We were grateful that our fellow missionaries also considered us fellow-laborers, partners in *the* great task.

12

Different Shapes and Sizes

Sentani was becoming more and more a home, a place for recharging and renewing our physical, emotional and spiritual energies. Prayer meetings and Sunday services held in various homes provided warm fellowship and inspiration, with various ones taking part. We sang to the accompaniment of a portable pump organ, the kind Elaine had played in Sharon, Pennsylvania, when her father conducted street meetings.

We were grateful for the friendship of the missionary families on the Hill. Although we all had our own particular schedules, we knew that we could count on the others to share in our joys and our sorrows.

In the four years between 1953 and 1957, the Alliance missionary force on the island grew from nineteen to forty-six. They arrived either by ocean freighter or airliner. Their first but temporary home was at Sentani as they prepared to move on to the interior. Those of us who lived on Mission Hill shared the responsibilities of providing housing and meals to anyone in transit.

One of our neighbors was Jerry Rose. Jerry was what one might call a "professional scrounger." He had the knack of being able to secure items of all kinds for himself and the Mission, all of which greatly improved life whether in "civilization" on the coast or in the interior.

If a generator was needed, Jerry either had one or knew where to get one. He also bought a refrigerated van trailer at Sentani for communal use. Such resourcefulness, of course, attracted the admiration of some and the criticism of others.

However one viewed him, all agreed that Jerry did things in a big way. He was far ahead of his fellow missionaries in developing local resources, starting agricultural projects, planning major station development, buying vehicles and communications equipment and funding their maintenance. Even in the earliest days in the Baliem, Jerry was already thinking ahead to schools and roads and telephone service before others had thought much beyond setting foot in the interior and learning a language.

On any mission field a tension exists between the proponents of a spartan simplicity and the proponents of a substantial infrastructure. Jerry leaned toward the latter. As one surveys the history of the development of Irian Jaya at the turn of the millennium, it is fair to say that many of the ideas Jerry was trying to carry out in the early '50s are now being adopted.

One of Jerry's projects was the introduction of horses and cattle to highland areas. On one occasion, he chartered the Sealand to transport a bull from Biak to Lake Tigi where he was assisting Kapaukus in starting a farm. The bull was a huge animal. With its enormous weight, it made almost a full load for the plane.

Before the flight, Jerry had administered shots to tranquilize the bull. All went well until about halfway to the Lakes, when the beast began to recover. Its struggle could be felt throughout the plane. He had been well tied, but managed to work his front legs free and began kicking. At one point, we feared it would break through the side walls or cause even more serious damage. The last half of the flight was on a wing and a prayer.

By the time we got to Lake Tigi, the bull was almost completely recovered and had no intentions of being off-loaded onto a raft. When the deed was finally accomplished, I was very relieved! But that was not the only trip in the Sealand which involved nonhuman creatures. Another flight was equally memorable.

One morning, I was taxiing toward the takeoff end of the Sentani runway when I increased power beyond normal. Suddenly, there was a loud bang, and the plane stopped moving. I managed to shut down the engines and got out. Light smoke was drifting up from one of the wheels. Instead of operating normally, an inflatable unit in the braking system had ruptured. We discovered that some wasps, trying to build a nest, had plugged the air relief lines with mud. We cleaned out the line, and the problem was solved.

Occasionally, native people from the highlands had opportunity to fly to the coast and have such worldview-altering experiences as seeing cars, plumbing, electric lights and ocean freighters for the first time. One such passenger was a colorful character named Ukumhearik. Elaine explains:

> Ukumhearik was a very important Dani leader, known and feared by many in the valley. After his younger brother broke his leg and was airlifted in the Sealand to Sentani for medical treatment, Ukumhearik wanted his turn for a trip to the coast.
>
> What he saw "outside" was almost too much for him. One great surprise was the ocean with its salty water. In the valley, salt was obtained with great effort. When Ukumhearik waded into the sea and then tasted that wonderfully salty water, he literally lapped it up and had to be restrained. When he went to the government's experimental farm and saw the big fat pigs, he scratched his head

and claimed that there could not be such animals. He loved to sit in our Land Rover with Lynne, who was just a toddler at the time. He seemed a gentle giant; it was hard to picture him as the most powerful man in the lower Baliem Valley.

Missionary children, too, who had been raised in the interior, were often wide-eyed at the world beyond the mountains and valleys. On one occasion, young Kathleen Gibbons and her family were leaving the Wissel Lakes for a short vacation. After landing at Biak and getting her first real view of the outside world, all she could say was, "Oh, the junk of things!"

An increasingly vital role we filled at Sentani was that of keeping the missionaries living in the remote interior supplied with food, equipment, mail and other supplies. Many hours were spent driving to and from Hollandia, with long shopping lists dictated during our scheduled radio contacts. Small as it was, Hollandia was a seaport and the government center for a large area. Its shops and warehouses provided just about anything one desired.

A typical trip into town might involve stops at the hardware store, DeBoer's bakery, a food importing warehouse, the post office and perhaps even a visit to a government office to process some paperwork. Around 1963, a group of missions, under the leadership of Harold Catto, who by that time had become the Alliance field chairman, formed a corporation called TMF

(The Missions Fellowship) to purchase and stockpile equipment and supplies in bulk. A warehouse in Sentani supplemented the hangar warehouse with its bins designated for each station.

Then, of course, there was the actual assembly of the cargo. Preparing a load for an aircraft is not like throwing things into a station wagon for a vacation trip. Sometimes, for example, one relatively heavy but small piece of equipment was all that would fit on a load. Tying down the cargo with nets or roping or webbed belts was also critical; a load shifting in flight could literally make the airplane impossible to fly.

When an airdrop was scheduled, the work of loading became even more exacting. Making up such a load is a complex process. Each piece needs to be light enough for the "pusher" to lift out the door of the moving plane while still maintaining his balance. Dick rigged up some fifty-five-gallon steel drums with a strong metal band fitted inside and secured by two mounting bolts with rings on the outside for attaching the parachute. These worked well.

Long before they built a landing strip at Homeyo, Bill and Gracie Cutts received their supplies by parachute drops. Because of the mountains surrounding the station, flying a drop pattern was difficult. On one memorable trip, Ken and Dick assisted in discharging the drums. It was just before Christmas, and the Cutts had ordered a kitten for their son Johnny. We carefully packed it in one of the drums.

Knowing that a dead kitten would be far worse than no kitten at all, we placed the kitten in a strong towel-lined cardboard box the size of a large shoe box. It, in turn, was surrounded by softer things—such as paper products, mail and cloth to be used as payment for the airstrip work—at the top of the fifty-five-gallon steel drum. As we closed the lid of the drum just before the drop, we could hear the kitten mewing softly. Thankfully, Johnny received his Christmas present—alive and well. He named the kitten Sputnik in honor of his incredible time in "space."

Weekends were a mixture of activities different from our weekday tasks. Sometimes, of course, bad weather during the week might mean we would make a flight on a Saturday, but usually Saturdays were days for family activities, projects around the house, trips to the beach. One of our favorites was near a World War II post beyond Hollandia called "Base G;" another, a swimming hole in a river running from Cyclops Mountain, where a large pool of icy water about four feet deep provided delightful respite from Sentani's heat.

Although we had four hours of electricity a day, running water and access to stores, living in Sentani was not always as civilized as one might expect. The simplest everyday tasks were often complicated and challenging. Elaine explains:

> All our laundry was done by hand (mine), and I washed every day to avoid a pileup of grubby, sweaty clothes. Not only would the quantity be overwhelming if left too long, but the damp clothes would have been ruined if left in the hot, humid environment. When I realized that hand action alone would not get the dirt out of Ed's work clothes and Ted's play clothes, I found a scrub brush and a piece of a plank which served as a washboard. Bar soap—elbow grease—cold water—*voila!*—clean clothes! Imagine my delight about a year into our term there when we were given a wringer washer.

Cooking and preparing food could be a challenge, too, and required some ingenuity. We had a three-burner kerosene stove, with a box-like "oven" that was placed over one burner. Not only was the stove limited in capacity, the food supply was limited in variety. In the early years at Sentani, we ate mostly canned food and rice, bananas, papaya, our own version of Jell-o made from Kool-aid, ice cream made in our kerosene refrigerator, cakes, pies and cookies. We made occasions for celebrating the simplest events.

When we invited Dutch or Australian friends for a meal, it was important that we state the exact time, as our terms and theirs were different. A Dutch couple would interpret "dinner" as the noon meal. To the Australians, "supper" was a late evening "spread," and the evening meal was "tea."

One Christmas, Dick came to our house dressed as Santa Claus. Lynne was not yet three years old, and she was a bit uncertain when he asked her to sit on his lap.

"Lynne," he said, once she had crawled up, "have you been a good girl this year?" Lynne started to cry and ran to Elaine.

"Oh, Mommy, what shall I say?" she asked through her tears.

Life was not always easy for our wives in other ways as well. While Al and I were flying, sometimes separately, sometimes together, they monitored our radio transmissions. There was, at times, plenty of reason to worry—and to pray.

On one occasion I was alone, flying supplies from Biak to Lake Paniai, when both engines began to misfire. I was about fifteen minutes from the mainland at a point where I needed to begin my climb over the pass into the Lakes; I knew that climbing to that altitude with engines that were not running properly could precipitate a serious problem.

To my left was a wide river that emptied into the sea. I decided to attempt a landing far enough upstream to allow the plane to drift toward the mouth of the river. I landed, shut down the engines and proceeded to climb up on the slippery aluminum wing to where the engine nacelles flowed into it. I cleaned the oil off the magnetos, secured the covers and returned to the cockpit.

By now, the plane had drifted about a half mile, but was still in the center of the river. I restarted the engines and prepared for takeoff. Thankfully, the engines ran smoothly, and I arrived safely at the Wissel Lakes.

Then, in November 1954, although the plane was scheduled for a major overhaul, I was asked if we could make an emergency trip to the Baliem. There were several reasons. The Kapauku workers, who had accompanied the initial party into the valley, were fearful of Dani reprisals and were threatening to desert. Also, I had taken in a group of government officials a week earlier and would bring them out one at a time. We would also pick up a pile of letters Lloyd and Myron had been writing but had no way to mail.

The day after a heavy rain, Dick and I decided to make the flight. Even with the river now at its highest level, it would be impossible to take off safely with more than 300 pounds of cargo or passengers aboard.

Usually after heavy rains, when the river rises quickly, large gravel bars form, sometimes just under the water's surface. This was what had happened during the sudden rise of the river the day before our departure.

We picked up our first load—a government official and all the mail—and, while taxiing upriver, noticed a number of new currents. About halfway to the turnaround point, we felt a bump through the hull. Dick rushed aft and removed sections of flooring. No visual damage. He gave the signal that all was OK. So I turned the plane around and repositioned for the takeoff run.

All was going well until we passed the initial trouble spot. By this point we should have been high in the water ready to lift into the air. Instead, for reasons unknown, we were bogged down, our hull dragging noisily in the water. Once I realized we were not in a position for a safe takeoff, I cut the power and threw the propellers into reverse to keep us from crashing into the bank at the turn.

"We're sinking!" Dick hollered from his position on the floor. Another split-second decision was needed. Beaching ourselves on the brush-covered bank seemed to be our only hope.

I rammed the throttles forward, and we plowed onto the bank, climbing it far enough to remain safely stuck. We got out to inspect the damage. Jerry Rose, who had been watching all this from the bank, dived under the plane and soon resurfaced with the news that the hull had ruptured at the point of the step. After much bailing, we were able to slow the flow of water by stuffing rags into the hole and furiously pumping.

One way or the other, we had to get the plane out of the valley. Should the river rise just a few feet more, it could swamp the plane, and we would have to abandon it. Apart from the loss of the plane, we would all be stranded in the valley. Our only option was to try to take off.

The three of us climbed aboard and each took up his duties. The government official, resplendent in his white dress uniform, lay on his stomach on the muddy floor and held the waste rag in the rupture. Dick stood at the rear door pumping the bilge water overboard.

The upriver taxi went fine, but we were less successful on the takeoff run. Almost to the bend, the plane still would not go up on the step. I was just about to abort the takeoff when I felt the step come into play. Now I had more control. With less hull in the water, lighter control pressures were needed to steer the plane. We entered the straight stretch and, after using more than half of it, became airborne. As we climbed away, water draining from the gap in the hull streamed behind us.

We had taken a big gamble. But the option simply was not acceptable. We would have risked the complete loss of the plane had we left it beached on the bank of that fickle river.

In some ways, the future of Alliance missions in New Guinea at that moment hinged on a split-second decision to beach the aircraft that otherwise would have sunk in the middle of the Baliem River. Since most of the banks of the Baliem are cliff-like walls of mud, God had provided a suitable one at that moment. He had intervened. The hope of reaching the people of Shangri-la was still alive and well.

13

Willing to Pay the Price

In February 1955, my family and I departed for the States for a brief furlough. Al and Mary Lewis returned to Sentani the day we left. Al resumed flying the Sealand, continuing our supply line to both the Baliem Valley and the Wissel Lakes.

While in the States, I was asked to report on our aviation ministry at that year's General Council meeting in Philadelphia. I included the following statistics in my report:

> During its 15 months serving the New Guinea field, the plane carried 87 tons of supplies and building materials—12 ½ tons were dropped; over 300 passengers were carried, and over $3,500 was earned in outside charters—mostly to other mis-

sion agencies. Over 160 round-trip flights were made into the Baliem and Wissel Lakes stations.

That same Council week, Ken Troutman, the board representative in New Guinea, sent this telegram to our New York headquarters: "LEWIS DEPARTED SENTANI APRIL 28, 8:40 STOP LAST REPORT OVER IDENBURG 9:20 STOP 6 DAYS SEARCH IN IDENBURG REVEALED NOTHING STOP."

Al Lewis and the Sealand were missing!

Dave Steiger, a pilot with MAF had been flying supplies to missionaries in the Bird's Head area of New Guinea that morning and heard Al's last radio call a few minutes after the one from the Idenburg.

"It's as black up here as my left eye," Al said. That was a reference to an injury he had received a few days earlier while cranking the stubborn diesel generator up on Mission Hill. He had slipped on some oil on the floor and hit his cheekbone on the generator.

The preceding month had been a busy one, including a complete engine overhaul and a backlog of freight to be delivered. Because the river level would soon be too low for landings in the Baliem, every day of flying was vital. Those pressures seem to have prompted his flight on April 28, 1955 in less than satisfactory weather.

A few days earlier, Myron Bromley had flown out to the coast for some dental work:

> At the end of April, 1955, I needed to visit a dentist, so I went to the coast for

the first time since we had entered the Baliem. With me went Yameke, younger half brother of Ukumhearik, the extremely important leader who had welcomed us into the valley. Ed and Elaine [Ulrich] were now gone, so Yameke and I slept in their house and ate our meals with Al and Mary Lewis.

Back in the Baliem, Yameke's mother was very upset about the disappearance of her son, and though she heard him try to reassure her over the radio, she would not be consoled. The decision was made for him to return home the next day. That was the last Sealand flight to land in the Baliem.

Coming back from my Hollandia dentist appointment on the 28th, I saw the empty hangar and heard the grim news that the Sealand was missing from its flight that morning, the only flight Al had made to the Baliem with no one else on board.

Dick detailed his last days with Al and the subsequent search in a letter to Alliance headquarters:

Al and I had been working on the engines for about three weeks and completed them on Friday, April 22. April 23rd we began our first trip of a series to the Baliem, trying to get caught up on our work, as well as stocking ahead on food and building materials. We made trips Saturday, Monday, Tuesday and Wednesday. Wednesday, Al suggested that I stay in overnight for a little change. Just before he took off for Sentani, he said that, if I liked, I could stay over two nights in the Baliem instead of just one.

Thursday, April 28, Al left Sentani alone. This was the first trip that he had made alone since he returned from furlough. When he didn't arrive in the Baliem around 10 o'clock, I was not concerned because I thought he went back to Sentani because of the weather.

It wasn't until I saw a Catalina coming in over the ridge late that afternoon that I realized the Sealand was missing. I told the other missionaries that the Sealand must be missing, that the Catalina was searching for it; but they said it was just flying around. I waited for some time, and finally it came into the Baliem. After they located our camp, they dropped a message for us to contact Sentani immediately. We could not transmit any message that night, but were able to receive enough to realize what had happened. The next morning, we made contact at 5 o'clock and learned that Al and the plane were missing. I requested that the government Beaver as well as MAF enter into the search with the Catalina.

April 29, the Catalina (whose crew was

> a little afraid of the high mountains) searched the entire Idenburg River area. The MAF plane returned . . . late that afternoon. All day we stayed by the radio in the Baliem, giving information to the Catalina as to the most likely area where the plane might be.
>
> On April 30, the MAF Pacer . . . came into the crash area. . . . We continued to search for about thirty minutes, then returned to Sentani. The Catalina continued searching over the Idenburg River that day. Later that afternoon I got together with the crews . . . to organize the search more efficiently so that we would know we had covered every area possible, and brief them on the most likely spots to be searched.

The next morning, the three planes left about 6:30 to cover the designated areas. The course generally flown from Sentani is 227°, which brings aircraft at a moderate altitude through that natural gap into the Baliem Valley. Lenehan and a Dutch pilot flew the route in a DeHavilland Beaver at exactly 227°, arrived at the Baliem Pass, and then flew back and forth, north and south then east and west, for about two-and-a-half hours.

Meanwhile, the Catalina searched the valley of the Hablifoeri River going four to five miles on a crisscross course on either side of the river until it empties into the Idenburg River. Following that, they spent the rest of the day flying around inside the Baliem Valley itself. Some searchers speculated that Al could be in the valley but unable to make radio contact.

During this time, MAF's Piper Pacer was searching Mud Pass to the west. After the men in the Beaver completed searching the pass itself, they left that area and worked eastward back to the pass, once again crisscrossing the terrain to check it from all angles. The Beaver then started on the ridges and worked down. Since the Beaver's engine had more than the maximum hours on it before the scheduled overhaul, Lenehan and the pilot were somewhat handicapped by not being able to inspect the higher ridges.

Three hours after the men took off from Sentani, the clouds were beginning to form, diminishing visibility. By then they estimated that only about half of the area was visible from the plane, the rest obscured by clouds.

Weather conditions got so bad that they were forced to leave the higher ridges and concentrate on the lower areas. Finally ending their search southeast of the Baliem, they returned to the valley and skirted the whole northern ridge in case the plane had spilled over into the next pass. Lenehan's letter continues:

> We arrived back in Sentani at 12:30, six hours after takeoff. The Pacer had made a stop in the Baliem to pick up one of the MAF pilots who stayed in over-

> night when I came out. They arrived back in Sentani about the same time. The Navy Catalina and Beaver both returned to Biak later that day, after informing us that, as far as they were concerned, the search was completed. The Catalina had spent as much as twelve hours a day searching for three full days, plus Thursday afternoon. Having complete charge of the Air-Sea Rescue work, their decision was final.

This was a discouraging turn of events for the missionary pilots and other civilian searchers, but it did not deter them from continuing to pray and think about ways to find Al and the Sealand.

On May 2, Charlie Mellis (an MAF pilot) and Dave went back to the pass and its ridges. Dick spent all morning at the air radio station in Sentani "flight following"—keeping in touch with Charlie so his position would be known in case something happened. Everyone in the air was being very cautious, neglecting no part of aviation safety and carefully watching out for each other.

Being at the radio shack also gave Dick access to the weather reports prior to the accident. Between contacts from the Pacer, Dick pored over the reports and began developing some theories. He found that a front had been over the area for about a week before the incident. On that particular day, it had cleared out sometime between 11 o'clock and midafternoon. This could only have been possible with a west wind, Lenehan surmised, because of the new position of the front and other data. Checking further, he found that the winds could have been up to twenty-five knots per hour (thirty miles). Chances were more likely that they had been about eight knots per hour, westerly wind.

Lenehan wrote:

> Since Al had taken off in very bad weather (the field had been closed for a short period prior to takeoff) and the dispatcher stated that Al disappeared in clouds over the field at about 300 meters, that indicated poor conditions to begin with. His first position report was light rain, flying at 9,000 feet, operation normal. His next reporting position point was the Idenburg River, and the report was still light rain, flying at 9,000 feet, operation normal. This report was received 43 minutes after he left Sentani.
>
> This would be approximately five minutes sooner than he should have arrived there. From this I felt he could have misjudged his ordinary track and drifted to the east considerably [to a place where the Idenburg's loops are much closer to Sentani, indicating that he was already off course this early in the flight].

Dick contacted the Civil Aviation Department. They contacted the governor, and the governor requested a meeting with Dick and Ken Troutman. There, Dick presented his case that the search should be resumed. The governor agreed, and the next morning the Catalina left Biak again on its way to the area.

In a pilots' meeting about noon that day, the Navy navigator helped plot some new search strategies, now using Lenehan's wind estimates. They mapped out an area to the east of the usual flight path to the Baliem and agreed to cover it more completely. Dick continues:

> All during this time much prayer had been made for good clear weather and that the plane would be found. We had the best weather I have ever seen on the ridges every day for several hours early in the morning. The Catalina agreed to leave Sentani at 5:30 the following morning, before daylight. The Pacer was retired the afternoon of May 3, and wouldn't fly the next day, for pilot rest and so the plane could be inspected.
>
> That night we received a cablegram from Ed to give consideration for easterly drift. We felt at that time that that was God's answer and that Al would be found the next day.
>
> On May 4, I went on the Catalina . . . to search this squared-off area to the east of the Baliem Pass. We covered it very methodically. There was one spot that I was not positive what it was. Even at the

> time I was convinced that it may have been rocks. We went as high in the Catalina as we safely could and covered all the area except the high ridge itself. We returned to Sentani about 11:15 and met with Mr. Visser (acting director of Civil Aviation), as I felt the one spot and the top ridge still had to be covered. The Navy said that the ridge was too high for the Catalina, and again called off the search operation!

The next day, the government, no doubt thinking the conditions too dangerous for a small plane, grounded the MAF plane for any further search in the Baliem Pass area. The Rose and Van Stone families requested that their women and children be evacuated from the Baliem, so Darlene and Bruce Rose, and Dorie and Bernie Van Stone were flown to Sentani. With official support withdrawn, and with the government's Beaver unable to fly high enough to reach the spot in question, the searchers spent their time following other leads.

From May 6 to 21, they followed up on a rumor that the Sealand may have crashed into Lake Sentani. When a search by divers turned up nothing, Lenehan once again requested that the government check the one spot on the ridge that had not been examined. "They said they had no planes to fly high enough, which actually was true," Dick reported.

Then he asked for permission to call in a United States Air Force plane from Manila or an Australian plane from Papua, New Guinea, but the Dutch civil aviation officials insisted it should be handled by the Dutch government. Nothing was done.

On May 27, Dick learned that an Australian plane on a special charter hop was at Sorong, an oil exploration region on the far western tip of New Guinea. He went to the radio shack and contacted the pilot to see if he would make a special flight for us into this ridge area.

To Dick's surprise, the pilot said he would do it if the Alliance could get government approval. Mr. Hamers, the director of Civil Aviation, approved the flight. So, at dusk on a Friday, the Australian plane arrived in Sentani. Lenehan describes the next day:

> May 28 was a notable day for us: our one-year anniversary on the field, and one month to the day from the accident. We took off at 6:10 in the chartered Avro Anson. The pilot, Charlie Mellis, Ken Troutman, Dr. Ebbinge and I were in the plane. We flew into the pass and made a left turn, checking the high ridges to the east of the pass. Then I had the pilot make a left turn, going away from the Baliem toward the high ridge. We were flying at 13,300 feet. As we went over the top of the ridge, I saw something white on an area of stone. Checking it with the

binoculars, I could recognize sheets of aluminum that were part of the load the day the plane was lost.

As the pilot carefully flew along these ridges, Dick and the others trained their binoculars on the limestone cliffs. The Sealand wreckage was partly hidden in the white rock formations:

> We all positively identified the airplane, as we made several maneuvers to get into position with full flap and gliding steep turns to get the plane about 400 feet over the Sealand. The pilot had to start at about 11,000 feet, making several "S" turns, passing over the airplane in a turn to the right, then a quick turn to the left to get out of the valley that the Sealand is caught in. We estimate that it is at about 10,000 to 10,300 feet altitude.

Dick took pictures of the plane each time they passed over it. Before he could spend time examining it without taking pictures, clouds began to form on the ridges. They had to leave the area.

As soon as he arrived at Sentani, he had the film developed and enlarged. That evening, he called a meeting with Mr. Hamers and Mr. Visser. They took the pictures, along with the maps Lenehan and other had drawn of the crash location, to the governor in Hollandia. There, they proposed a ground-based operation for a party to go in both to recover Al's body and to more closely examine the plane. Such an expedition would require military support and involve the cooperation of government personnel in various departments. No hope was held for Al's survival. Lenehan explained:

> To see the airplane as we did makes one realize that Al never could have known he hit anything. Death would have been instantaneous. He hit solid rock at a high speed.
>
> Whether anything was wrong with the airplane, we do not know, but we feel certain it is a condition caused by instrument flying, both because he was off course about five miles to the east, and that the ridge is over 1,000 feet higher than his flight plan called for.

So on May 28, exactly a month after its disappearance, the Sealand was found. However, it would be more than four years before the crash site would be reached on foot. One attempt to do so was made in 1958, described in a letter to Alliance headquarters from Jerry Rose:

> I will not burden you with a long report of an unsuccessful trip. Suffice it to say that we were gone thirteen days on the trip to the Sealand crash. Four of these days we worked out of a base camp trying to find a route up the steep, slippery limestone cliffs. After four days our supplies demanded that we begin the return trip.

> A later flight showed that we were less than a mile from the wreck and perhaps a few more days would have been sufficient to find a way.

In December, 1959, Jerry Rose and nineteen others reached the crash site. Harold Catto described their discovery of the wreckage in an article for the *Alliance Witness*:

> We arrived at the plane around half past four. What a shambles! It is no wonder it was difficult to figure out how things lie from the air, for pieces are scattered all over the side of the mountain. The main part of the plane is lying in a hole some three to four hundred feet beyond the first point of impact and perhaps fifty feet lower.
>
> It would appear that the plane was in a climb, for the tail wheel section, left pontoon and some of the things that were carried in the tail section are in a crevasse on the outside of the ridge. There is no sign of fire anywhere. The aluminum sheets of the cargo are some two hundred feet farther up the mountain from the plane, about six hundred feet from the first impact. . . .
>
> The actual resting place of the plane is at 10,400 feet, as recorded by the two altimeters carried by the party.

The body of Mr. Lewis was found in the upper part of the cockpit. In a letter to Mr. Chrisman, Area Secretary. Harold Catto further describes the event:

> The plane surely is a shambles, spread all over the mountainside like a bottle when you smash it against a rock. Al never knew what happened, so if we had gotten there the day of the wreck we could have done no more than we did now. It was impossible to bury the body in the ground as there is just not enough soil. So we placed it in a drum and put it into one of the crevasses in the rock right underneath the cockpit of the plane.

Before the party left for the trip, Mary Lewis, Al's wife, asked Harold to bring back Al's watch and wedding ring. Once at the site, Harold told the group not to disturb the area since he first wanted to search for the ring and watch. Harold continues:

> I went to the plane and to the cockpit to see if I could find them. They were nowhere around since the flesh was gone from Al's hands. I crawled out and went underneath to see if I could see anything there. I soon realized that the plane was sitting right over a big crevice. As I looked around, I saw about three blades of grass sticking out of the rock. There, hanging on one of the blades was the

> wedding ring! Imagine, after four years, it was still hanging there.

The watch was never found.

On Sunday morning, December 20, 1959, Harold Catto and the other men arranged some sheets of the roofing aluminum from the cargo in the shape of a giant cross on the mountainside, then held a burial service. Catto continues:

> After the committal, Mr. Gonsalves (a Dutch official), unfurled the Dutch flag and in the name of the government of New Guinea named the mountain Lewis Top.
>
> Thus closes this chapter in the life of our beloved missionary brother, but we await the return of our Lord to be united again and to see the results of his "total committal" in giving his life for the advance of the gospel in the Baliem Valley.

Al's body rested there until a day in 1991 when it was carried to Wamena by a team organized by a pastor from a local Alliance church. He had reported to the missionaries that tourists were disturbing the wreckage, and he arranged for the body to be brought to Wamena for burial in the large cemetery there. In 1993, the Alliance would name its Bible school in Elelim, a station within sight of the rocky ranges of Pass Valley, the Albert Lewis Bible School.

"It is going to cost, I know," Al had once written of his missionary commitment, "but I am willing to pay the price."

14

Journey into the Unknown

With the Sealand destroyed, it was clear that future flying in New Guinea would be mainly with land planes, not primarily seaplanes. Even at the time of this writing, MAF operates only one floatplane in Irian Jaya.

In the very early days, MAF's floatplane serviced some highland stations and sometimes supplied and evacuated our missionaries after the Sealand's loss. Now, it was obvious that the aviation program of the Alliance needed to change, as Myron Bromley later summarized:

> Meanwhile the Mission, consulting with Ed, chose to replace the Sealand amphibian with a much smaller but very versatile Cessna aircraft which could land on a high altitude airstrip less than

> five hundred yards long. Immediately, Lloyd and Jerry began to work on an airstrip very close to the Hetigima house site Lloyd had chosen. By July, the airstrip was ready for the first landing.
>
> Ed and Elaine returned to the field, Ed as pilot of the Cessna and head of the Alliance aviation program there. He brought that plane in for its first Baliem landing and kept us supplied.

During our furlough, MAF had assisted me in some needed training to maximize the effectiveness of our program. Since I had never flown from short mountain airstrips, I went through an accelerated program with MAF in Fullerton, California, a version of the course all MAF pilots take as part of their orientation.

In a Cessna identical to the one that was then being shipped to our field, I practiced approaches to short, high, narrow airstrips in tight canyons among California's Sierra Madre ranges, learned more about weather avoidance maneuvers and studied engine management techniques for the Continental engine in the Cessna, a very different power plant from the Rolls Royce Gipsy engines that the Sealand had used.

Back in New Guinea, I worked hard to reestablish a supply route to our stations in the Baliem and other highland areas. While the Cessna 180 was on its way to Hollandia, the missionaries in the Baliem constructed a 1,200 foot runway with about a 10° slope up the side of a mountain. In early October, within five months after the Sealand crash, our new Cessna also landed at Hetigima. An October 1955 report, written by Ken Troutman, shares the joy of that day:

> The arrival of the new Cessna 180 has been a cause for real praise. Truly God has done the impossible. Right after the crash of our Short Sealand plane, when visiting some of the government officials and the Navy commander, the question was asked as to how long we would be without a plane. The answer that it would probably be five months was very amusing to them, as nothing has ever happened that fast here in New Guinea. They were very pessimistic and assured me that we most likely would have to rely upon them for at least eight months to a year. . . . However, God has undertaken and the new plane was here in New Guinea taking care of our needs in just four months.

It was clear that this new perspective on Mission aviation in New Guinea would have some far-reaching effects. Ken explains:

> With the Cessna 180, God is leading us in an entirely different approach to the transportation problem in New Guinea. After the first landing on the strip in the

> Baliem, things began to happen. Our eyes were turned to the possibility of strips in other places. This is possible as strips for a small plane do not have to be as long or hard as for larger planes. . . . With the possibility of Nabire being used, work was immediately begun on the strip at Obano on Lake Paniai and in three weeks' time the first successful landing was made.
>
> Our attention is now focused upon our Moni station at Homeyo, and we hope to see a strip there before long. We feel that now God is leading us to the Uhunduni people who until now have appeared impossible to reach. It is quite certain that a strip can also be built in the Ilaga Valley. We pray that, by the use of the Cessna 180 plane, we will be able to reach every one of the four tribes for which we are responsible.

This report expressed a hope that would soon come to fruition. During the two years after that first Baliem strip was opened, more than fifteen strips were completed throughout the highlands. All were built by the missionaries with whatever local help they could get. Of course, a major problem was getting to the airstrip site in the first place, establishing good relations with the local people and then getting to work.

After the Hetigima airstrip had been built and regular supply by air had helped the missionaries develop a major base there, they turned their consideration to expanding into other areas of the Baliem Valley. It was on early expeditions from Hetigima that the missionaries encountered hostile Dani and harrowing travel difficulties as well.

Another complication was the discovery of several distinct dialects of the Dani language in the Baliem. This meant that eventually it would be necessary to do three different translations of the New Testament in that area. It was a few years later that the wisdom of this decision to expand into new areas of the valley became clear. Dani groups farther north in the valley proved to be much more receptive to the gospel than those where we first landed.

Some of the early valley explorations were on foot. A large network of trails used by intergroup traders crisscrossed the valley. Since much of the valley was fairly flat and grassy, a lot of ground could be covered in one day. The Baliem River offered another route for travelers. Cargo on an early Sealand flight had included the parts for a motorboat. Jerry Rose brought back a fifteen-horsepower Mercury outboard from the States.

On the day the Sealand crashed, Dick had remained in the Baliem with Jerry and Lloyd and joined them on a trip up the Baliem River and into a tributary stream called the Aikhe. While two of them were visiting a village on the banks of the river, angry villagers chased them back to the boat and began firing arrows as they ran.

After the missionaries were back in the boat and fleeing downriver, Lloyd discovered that the pain in his leg was not from brushing against a shrub while running, but from a Dani arrow with a barbed hardwood point that had lodged deeply in his thigh. He carefully removed it when he returned to Hetigima. We would soon find out, however, that Dani arrows were not the only dangers on Baliem River boat trips.

One week in 1956, I was invited to join the missionaries on a trip upriver to search for suitable airstrip and station sites. A few weeks earlier, we had spotted a likely looking strip site in mid-valley near a bend in the river. Early in the morning, as the mist still hung on the brown water, we walked from the mission house at Hetigima, down the sloping hill to the dock where the boat was moored under overhanging casaurina trees. With us were several extra red tanks of gasoline to feed the motor, and three spare propellers, shearpins and other hardware that most people wouldn't think of taking along on a morning's boat ride. This after all, was no pleasure cruise, but a journey into the unknown.

As we made our way slowly upriver against a powerful current, we came to some shallow rapids. We noticed the motor jump a few times and nearly stall as the propeller began hitting large limestone rocks just beneath the surface. I moved further forward toward the bow of the heavily loaded boat to help raise the prop a little further out of the water. Suddenly, without warning, it struck another rock and was sheared off. Now without power, we began drifting backward down the river, rapidly picking up speed as white-water splashed around us.

Then the boat hit a large submerged rock and I was thrown into the raging water. Struggling to keep my head above water—particularly above the rocks—I found myself being pulled deeper and deeper into the cold, muddy water. Grazing large stones and trying my best to hold my breath, I finally surfaced about 100 feet downstream, gasping for air as I continued to be catapulted to where I did not know.

Unfortunately, the morning in the mile-high valley had been cool. I was wearing a heavy jacket and heavy shoes. Dressed like this, I knew I would have difficulty trying to swim even in calm water. Another 100 yards or so downriver, I noticed that the current was taking me near a fallen tree. With great effort, I swam toward it and was forced by the current into its branches. I clung there, gasping for breath and completely exhausted, fearing that, at that altitude and in that cold water, my minutes on earth were probably few. About that time, I was dragged back into the crippled boat, wet, cold and shivering.

We replaced the propeller with another one, fastening it with a shearpin from our little hardware supply. We proceeded on our perilous journey, but often were forced out of the boat to pull it through the shallow rapids. Turning off the engine and pulling the nearly empty boat through the water kept the propeller from further damage. Though the water we splashed through was bone-chilling cold, the party was surprisingly cheerful.

Around noon and now above the rapids and able to make good speed under power, we began passing various Dani villages spaced out along the banks of the river. At each settlement, we were invited to stop and spend some time. Our response, though it angered the Dani, was not to do this. The missionaries had learned on earlier trips that to stop could mean a delay of a day or more. The Dani, out of jealousy, would often prevent visitors leaving a village, preferring to have their company and trading goods instead of sharing with their neighbors.

After a few more miles of travel, this time in a relatively rock-free stretch of the river, another pin sheared off. Since the water here was flowing quietly, we were able to paddle to the shore and make the necessary repairs. As we did, we noticed that a large group of about 100 Dani warriors was assembling on a high ridge behind the opposite bank, their spears by their sides, their eyes riveted in our direction. What the next few moments would bring, we could not predict.

To further complicate the situation, the unexpected trouble in the rapids meant that we were down to our last shearpin, a makeshift one fashioned from a brass screw taken from the boat. As we refilled the main gas tanks, we realized that as this rate we could not reach the airstrip site by nightfall. We decided to return to Hetigima, where the Van Stones and Roses were based.

As we started back down the river, we noticed that the Dani men were running downriver too. The river pulled us quickly along, but the swift currents kept us busy avoiding shallows, logs and rocks. Suddenly, we caught sight of the villages where earlier we had been asked to stop. Many Dani warriors were now lining the river's edge. As we approached, they began shouting at us. We were thankful for the rapidly moving current, for it looked as though we would have to run the gauntlet.

As we swept past, we threw cowrie shells to the men, hoping to divert their attention. With motor roaring and spray splashing over the bow, we watched as long spears pierced the water just behind the boat. Soon we were past the last village. But more danger lay ahead.

Some Dani were still running, following us on our journey downstream. We figured that perhaps they had seen us flounder in the rapids that morning and were planning to accost us there.

We were right!

As soon as we reached the rapids, two warriors rushed down the bank to the river's edge, their spears held high, ready to hurl. For some reason, they did not throw them, and we bounded and bounced through the rapids. About two hours later, almost dusk, we pulled up at the small dock at Hetigima. It had been a journey we would not soon forget!

Later expeditions upriver resulted in the Mission successfully establishing stations and building airstrips at Pyramid, Tulem and Ibele.

Myron Bromley describes 1956 as a year of expansion of the work in the Baliem:

> The Bozemans, then the Youngs, then Ed Maxey arrived, and we probed up the Baliem River. Einar Mickelson, who had been chosen by the Mission board to head the Baliem section of the field, was part of our group as we finally pushed by boat, then foot, to the top of the Grand Valley, just above the mountain the Archbold party had appropriately named Pyramid.
>
> Ed Ulrich stayed at Hetigima with the airplane for a period and made drops to us of the gear we had left behind. As the plane swooped very low over the flat, grassy land below our Pyramid camp, all kinds of things were dropped. Mr. Mickelson radioed that he would like his toilet bag. When his similar Bolex movie camera bag was dropped instead, he covered his face with his hands and asked Lloyd to go check it! Amazingly, a push on the shutter button produced a smooth whir; the camera worked fine, a tribute to the makers and a skillful pilot.
>
> Although the large population around Pyramid included a number of people who felt no inhibitions about taking things from our camp, big groups worked hard on constructing the airstrip. It was finished in an amazingly short time, and

Ed made the first landing on August 27, 1956, thirteen months after the opening of the Hetigima airstrip.

From the air, Dani villages appeared like huge mushroom patches. At ground level, one enters a house on hands and knees through a narrow slit in the wall. The houses are round, the men's house at one end of the village square, the women's houses, along the sides, often built into the ends of long, low, rectangular buildings for cooking and keeping pigs. Once inside, one's eyes become accustomed to the semi-darkness. The low ceiling hangs just a few inches overhead. A smoldering fire burns in the center of the hut. Above the ceiling are the sleeping quarters, well heated during cold nights by the fire underneath.

Walls and ceiling are coated with a sticky black soot. Breathing is difficult, especially for strangers. Pork fat is the choice cut and is given to the honored guest. An average village may house from forty to eighty people, and perhaps twice as many highly prized pigs. Wealth is determined by the number of pigs and wives a man has. The more wives he has, the more gardens they can plant and the more pigs they can feed.

There was always an unexpected thrill in making the first landing on some newly completed strip. During the building, hundreds of Dani worked for months digging with sticks, carrying dirt by handfuls, never realizing the end result of what they were doing.

Finally, at a new airstrip, the day came for the first landing. Awestruck Dani gathered to see the great bird that carries people inside. After one such landing, hundreds of warriors surrounded the plane at a cautious distance, their long spears extended high above it. Once they got braver, they came closer until their long spears made an outline of the plane in much the same manner as the knife thrower outlines his subject.

At one station, the occasion for all the warriors to be present was that a great battle was in progress. Our first landing had interrupted it! "Time" was called while they inspected the plane. One warrior who had just been killed lay just a few feet off the end of the strip.

Highland wars sometimes followed such a pattern. One group would notify the other that they had come to fight, and a battle would begin. The combatants would approach to within a few hundred feet, but instead of shooting arrows directly, they danced in circles launching their arrows high into the air to fall among the enemy. After the battle had raged for a while, a halt would be called.

At that point, the women, who had been standing on the sidelines, rushed out to collect the arrows which had fallen short. With the field cleared, the battle resumed. At dusk, each side returned home. If a casualty occurred, the battle might continue until the score on both sides was the same.

But not all wars were so "civilized." Blitzing warriors often sacked a village, impaling victims by ramming their long spears through the grass houses and burning the whole community. It was not unusual to see several villages burning simultaneously.

How can one express the thrill of seeing mission stations grow in areas where for centuries spiritual darkness had held people in its deadly grip? These settlements provided gateways to human minds long imprisoned in superstition and ignorance. And none of them could be established in the highlands without the airstrips—and without the little airplanes and those who flew them.

Teamwork—that's what it took. That was—and is—God's plan.

15

Trouble!

Every airstrip in New Guinea was different. Some had been hacked out of rocky slopes, some were old garden lands with the ditches filled in, and some had been built by digging out as much as four feet of soft peat to reach a solid clay base. Still others were constructed by covering a peat base with a layer of clay a foot thick. The clay then baked like cement in the hot sun. On such a strip we had our first accident with a Cessna.

It took over a year of hard labor by Bill Cutts and a few Moni to build the strip on the edge of a cliff at Homeyo. The approach end to it was over a 1,500-foot ravine about two miles across. The strip began abruptly at the edge of the ravine and extended 1,200 feet to the wall of a mountain. Because of the deep bed of peat, where a six-foot stick could be pushed down out of sight, it was necessary to carry by hand thousands of heavy loads of good clay to make the surface a foot thick.

Finally, the strip was ready for the first landing. I made a few circles to reconnoiter it while talking to the missionary below by radio. My only passenger, the Director of Civil Aviation in New Guinea, and I tightened our seat belts, snugged our shoulder harnesses and radioed that we were ready to land. As we were low on the approach, still 1,500 feet above the torrential river below, the face of that mountain ahead of us looked much closer than the 1,200 feet it was.

We touched down and rolled 800 feet along the hard clay surface. It looked as though we had made it. Then, suddenly, the Cessna flipped onto its back in what seemed like a slow smooth motion. Mr. Hamers and I were held upside down by our seat belts and shoulder harnesses. Neither of us was injured during the flip-over, but releasing ourselves from the upside-down position was a precarious and delicate operation. Ironically, the ten dozen eggs that were part of the cargo were undamaged!

What caused this to happen? The answer was self-evident. Two deep ruts about twenty feet long revealed where the layer of clay topping was thinner than the rest. The plane's wheels had broken through the crust into the softer soil below.

The Moni at Homeyo, having never before seen a plane land, appeared surprised when we told them this was not a normal landing! With their help, we righted the aircraft and surveyed the damage. Both wings were bent, the roof section buckled, rivets sheared off and the tail assembly twisted. Also, from where it had flipped through the mud, the engine cowling was severely damaged, as were the propeller and the engine mounts.

Although the plane was far from a total loss, the distance from a repair facility would mean that it would be out of commission for quite some time. The trek from Homeyo to our headquarters station at Enarotali at the Wissel Lakes would take three days. There a government Beaver floatplane could pick us up and take us to Sentani for new parts and tools.

For Bill Cutts and his crew, it was back to work on the airstrip. After several months, MAF's Piper Pacer landed there with Dick, who recommended a plan for temporary repairs of the Cessna. Following weeks of labor and many hours pleading with officialdom, I was given permission to fly the crippled Cessna 300 miles over the mountains to Sentani for rebuilding.

Homeyo was not the only place where we had made an unconventional landing. An incident at Gakokebo on Lake Tigi proved to be equally unpredictable. Mary Catto relates the story from her viewpoint on the ground:

> Everyone was excited to think that today the airplane would land in Gakokebo! The entire village was waiting anxiously in the clearing. The plane touched down and

> started up the strip. All of a sudden it veered to the right and gracefully turned over on its back! I began to weep. We were all running toward the plane, but the women were trying to comfort me with, "Why are you crying, Mama? The plane is here!" They didn't know the difference. Who cares how it lands? It's here!
>
> Harold ran toward the plane, all the while trying to figure out what had happened. Seeing the gas spilling out, he drew a line around the plane and said, "No one is to cross over this line!" and "No one is to smoke!"
>
> One lady asked quietly, "Can I eat a sweet potato?"

Fortunately, the plane received little damage, and immediate modifications were made to prevent future problems with the parking brake.

The Homeyo incident prompted a new policy: new airstrips would be checked out via on-ground inspections by a pilot, not just from the air. With New Guinea's lack of roads, the approval of a new airstrip for a first landing usually meant a long walk for a pilot. Trekking became part of my job description! Not until the coming of an MAF helicopter to the island in 1972 would the job get any easier. Now, an airstrip can be inspected by a pilot flown in by helicopter in the early morning and inaugurated by a Cessna landing by the same pilot later that same day. But in the 1950's, long treks were the rule.

In the years while we flew the Sealand to and from the Wissel Lakes and Biak, we learned about an abandoned airstrip on the coast near Nabire. It had been used by the Japanese in World War II. Now, with our operations using land planes instead of the seaplane, it was time to think about secondary bases. Perhaps Nabire could be made operational again.

A ground survey of the site revealed several things. There would need to be extensive repair of the grass runway which lay pocked by several large bomb craters. Although some had been filled in, they were soft bogs. Mr. Garretson, a Dutchman who lived adjacent to the strip and traded in teakwood, explained that in order to repair a bomb crater, one first must dig out the soil at the bottom. Unless this is done, the soil compressed from the blast acts like the sides of a kettle, trapping water and causing a bog. If the compressed shell is dug through, the water can seep out and allow a solid fill. We built a storage building and a small shed for the pilot to sleep in.

The early days at this primitive base were eventful. All supplies arriving at Nabire came via ship from Biak. Since there was no dock for the ship, supplies were picked up at the anchored vessel and delivered to shore by native boats. Airplane fuel came in fifty-five-gallon drums. The full drums were dumped overboard into the sea. Because gasoline is lighter than water, the drums would float. We hired men to swim out and bring them to shore.

Nights alone in the "living quarters" sometimes provided more thrills than the flying to and from the interior, refueling, reloading, flying, refueling, over and over. On one occasion I was awakened by what sounded like a bulldozer just outside the thin plywood wall. I looked out to see about ten wild boars rooting up the ground around the camp. In the morning I found that almost every inch of soil was disturbed—some of it under the floor of my cabin.

Another night I was awakened by flapping noises. In the moonlight I saw several large, leathery-winged, prehistoric-looking birds flying around. Each had a long head and a wingspread of five to six feet. Whatever they were, they managed to do a good job of disturbing this missionary's sleep. (I later learned that they are called flying foxes and belong to the bat family.)

After a long day's work, it was very relaxing to take a swim. However, on one takeoff from the Nabire strip, I noticed a hammerhead shark lying in a shallow stream that entered the sea about 100 yards away from where we often took our refreshing swims! That kind of discouraged me from future dips.

Soon we received word that our second new Cessna had reached Sydney, Australia. Dick and our other pilot, Bill Paul, assembled the plane there and flew it to Hollandia. Bill and his family had arrived in Sentani a few month's earlier. Following the Sealand crash and Al's death, I had recommended the hiring of another pilot. Bill had been recruited. After the new Cessna arrived, I returned to the Wissel Lakes post to which I had walked after the accident at Homeyo, only this time it was in the new plane—and it was to a small strip at a settlement called Obano, on the edge of Lake Paniai, where a dedication service for the plane would be held that afternoon.

The service was not without complications. First, we waited several hours for the missionaries to arrive from Enarotali, twelve miles across the lake. Then, just at the end of the dedication service, heavy rains came. We all ran to take refuge in the newly completed school near the runway. Finally, after the rain eased, all of the missionary staff departed by boat for Enarotali, leaving the plane at the Obano strip.

The following day, Sunday, we heard that flashing lights, which appeared to be signals from mirrors across the lake, had been seen by Kapauku at Enarotali. Then, in the direction of the Obano strip, we observed heavy smoke. That usually meant houses burning. The big question on my mind, of course, was "What about the plane?"

We quickly notified the local chief of police and seven of us started across the lake in a police outboard. Heavy wind kicked waves up to four feet. We were almost swamped each time we smacked into one. About seven miles from Enarotali, we approached a small island and decided to climb to a high point for a better look at Obano, five miles away. From that vantage point, we could see that most of the houses in the village had been burned. We could also see the plane, still on the airstrip where we had left it, but could not tell if it had been damaged.

Should we continue on to Obano unarmed or return to Enarotali? From our lookout, we observed several native boats gathering along a point of land that lay between us and Obano. If we proceeded, would we be needlessly exposing our defenseless party to a mass attack? It seemed foolish to take the risk. The decision was made to return to Enarotali.

On the way, we overtook a party of Kapauku in a dugout canoe. They were covered with mud from head to foot—a sign of mourning. From them we learned that a number of the Indonesian staff of our school at Obano had been killed. These Kapauku, from Enarotali, had hidden in the tall grass and had managed to escape the spears and arrows of those who were fomenting this rebellion.

At 5 p.m., two boatloads of police and the local government controller left for Obano, a one-and-a-half-hour trip over the rough lake. Ken Troutman and I followed in a Mission boat. The police reached the opposite side of the lake ten minutes ahead of us and had already started up the twenty-minute-long trail to the airstrip and mission station. It was dark as we edged our boat up a small stream to reach the lower end of the trail.

When we stopped the outboard motor, we could hear the enemy dancing their victory ceremony on the mountain close by. We knew that our position at the end of the trail was, to put it mildly, precarious. Tall grass overhung both the stream and the trail. We were unarmed. Our long native-type boat was pointed the wrong way in the narrow stream. We decided that it would be futile to proceed up the trail in hope of contacting the police in the dark.

We turned the boat around and quietly slipped downstream to the lake. From there we could hear the shouts of the enemy as they taunted the police party. Then it began to rain torrentially as frequently it can in those highlands. Since we could be of no possible help, we decided to return to .

Plowing back through the waves and downpour of that pitch-black night, we had to pass the point of land where earlier we had watched some native boats gather. They could easily be upon us before we could see them and, of course, they could hear our outboard motor.

Just as we approached that point, we saw three flares fired by the police at Obano. Was it a signal to us? If so, what did it mean?

After a few minutes of prayer and thought, we decided that, since we were unarmed, we would stay with our original plan and continue to Enarotali. The police had enough room in their boats for any wounded. Even at our present position, we were extremely vulnerable.

Cold and wet, we reached Enarotali an hour later. It was not until after midnight that we knew we had made the right decision. The flares had been set off by the police as a signal that they were being flanked by the enemy and that each one should retreat to the boats as quickly as possible. The police later confirmed that nine people had been killed at Obano, and that the mission station and airplane had been destroyed.

The massacre was a great shock. Later that night, the missionaries were told to move into one house which could be more easily defended than several scattered ones. Together we recalled recent rumors circulating in the area. Some Kapauku were blaming the whites for the increasing mortality of their pigs. There was a pig epidemic which the government was doing its best to abate, but the Kapauku didn't understand.

Monday morning, we learned that the attack was to have been made on Saturday, the day we dedicated the plane, but because of the heavy rain it had been delayed. We had escaped death because of that intrusive rain!

The local police force mustered twenty men. Early Monday morning, they once again crossed the lake to Obano, but were unable to establish a base. The same day, we were warned that Enarotali was to be attacked at 10 o'clock the next morning by the people from Obano. This time, all Mission and government personnel moved into four houses that were in close proximity to each other. The Kapauku of Enarotali were assembled, and the chiefs passed out white bandages to be worn as head and arm bands to distinguish them from the enemy.

We learned too that it was not only the people from Obano we were fighting. The warriors from Obano had enlisted allies, great bands of people from every direction around Enarotali. Immediately after the attack at Obano, runners had set out with the severed fingers of the Indonesian teacher named Ruland Lesnussa. At each village, the runner offered the fingers to the elders. If they accepted, that village was an ally. This continued until Tuesday morning when almost all Kapauku within twenty miles of Enarotali had joined in the fight.

Our position was serious. The local people were very frightened. At one time, we decided to evacuate all women and children by Navy plane, but learned that the locals would take this as a sign of our expected defeat. In that case, they probably would defect to the side that appeared to be winning. After much prayer and discussion, the women of the Mission—Yvonne Heiden, Leona St. John, Elze Stringer, Marion Doble and Ken Troutman's wife, Vida—remained. Enarotali was literally ringed by warriors who could attack at any moment and from any side.

We were in hourly radio contact with our Sentani base and prayed together as well as in our own quiet times. We knew we were outnumbered and very vulnerable. The government station had also made contact with the outside. Although the government promised additional police, outsiders did not quite grasp the seriousness of the situation.

The mountainsides surrounding Enarotoli were already covered with hundreds of enemy forces. We watched with apprehension as their number grew in strength and they gradually worked down toward the valley that separated their mountain from our ridge. We had only six policemen, plus 300 to 400 Kapauku to protect Enarotali. The rest of them had sortied to Obano earlier in the morning.

At 9:50 a.m., the local constabulary completed their "waitai-ing" (war dancing) and moved out in tight groups to meet the enemy horde. I was in the radio room at the office waiting for the transmitter to warm up when I heard the first war cries. Because the Enarotali warriors had engaged the enemy in the open ground between the ridges, the police had to concentrate their fire on the opposite mountain slope.

I reported the battle action to Sentani until the battery ran down. When the base did not get my anticipated call the next hour, they presumed the station had fallen.

The battle in the valley was long and bitter, but the enemy did not break through. They finally withdrew. Perhaps the firing of the guns had confused them. However, there were few gunshot casualties, since the police could fire only against those on the mountain.

During the afternoon, a large Dutch Navy Martin "Mariner" flying boat arrived with sixteen policemen and supplies. The supplies were just as important as the policemen, since every bit of food had to be flown to the Lakes.

Tuesday night was another tension-filled time of standing watch. All during the night, we could hear the war cries of the enemy coming from the surrounding hills. An all-out attack at night could easily have been fatal. As dawn broke, more war cries came from the hills. Another attack seemed imminent.

Thankfully, the next morning, two more navy planes landed on the lake, with more police and supplies. Before each plane landed, the pilots flew over the gathered enemy, firing machine guns in warning. Gradually the mountainsides cleared.

Later in the day, the reinforced police gained a foothold on the shore at Obano, and we received permission to proceed there in order to confirm the loss of Mission property and plane and to identify the dead. It had been five days since the first attack, but the enemy had been so entrenched that it had been impossible for the police to retrieve the slain.

Harold Catto and I, accompanied by a police captain and seven troopers, set out for Obano. At the advance post on the edge of the lake, seven more men joined us, including the chief of police. The six officers had Sten machine guns; the rest carried carbines. Although by this time in New Guinea it had become Alliance policy that missionaries not carry firearms, Harold and I packed shotguns by order of the police. Behind us, from a ten-foot high platform, a policeman kept a Bren gun firing over our heads as we moved slowly down the trail.

From the mountains we could hear the enemy calling out our names as we marched along. The officers kept firing their machine guns into the tall grass on either side and ahead as we advanced. Sometimes we could see up the trail a few hundred feet and note the enemy darting off to either side into the tall grass. The trail led straight to the station, but paralleled the airstrip at a distance of about half a mile.

Ahead, where the station had stood, we could hear the enemy performing their war dances. We did not want to risk a mass attack. Since the airstrip was parallel to us at this point, we decided to cross to it through the deep grass.

We proceeded cautiously and slowly, the muddy ground sucking at our boots, the tall grass catching our clothing and hands. The police continued firing over our heads. It was a loud and suspense-filled hike, to say the least!

Finally, we reached the nearest end of the airstrip. At the opposite end, the warriors were still hammering and banging on the plane. Pieces of hacked aluminum flashed like mirrors even under the cloudy sky. Then a few shots in the air sent the men scattering for cover.

We walked up the strip, picking up instruments and pieces from the main section of the plane which lay hundreds of feet away. Parts of the cowling, tail, doors and fuselage were scattered everywhere. The interior was completely gutted and the beautiful red material from the upholstery would now be used for headdresses of warriors. While the police guarded me, I took some pictures.

I was shocked. Just two days earlier, this little Cessna 180 had been new and shiny, its aluminum skin buffed to a brilliant polish and its sides emblazoned with handsome stripes of black and bright red paint. Now, what had been tires were black twisted shreds of rubber on the muddy ground. The landing lights and all the windows had been smashed and the cowling chopped away from the engine. A large chunk of the fuselage just in front of the tail was missing, chopped into pieces.

The plane looked as if its back had been broken. Both of the doors and the baggage compartment door had been ripped off. The attackers had stolen the entire load of trade goods and food supplies that were to have been dropped to the missionaries at Ilaga the next day. One lime-green steel canister which contained fuel for the Ilaga, lay on its side on the ground, sunk partway into the mud.

The police made quick reconnaissance and decided not to enter the Mission area beside the airstrip without reinforcements, so we started back down the strip. Even before we reached the lower end, we could hear people once more hammering and chopping on the plane.

Our return through the deep grass to the trail was even more risky. As we crept along, insulting cries from the mountains called out the names of the next victims. While we had been gone from the advance post, it had been attacked from two sides and one policeman had been wounded by an arrow. It was late afternoon and raining when we started back to Enarotali.

By Saturday, three planeloads of Marines had arrived. Although modern firearms were an advantage, the government preferred not to use them as a direct means of fighting. The greatest losses suffered by the rebels were at the hands of the Enarotali warriors. While the guns kept the enemy in the mountains, our native allies had gone out and burned houses, slaughtered pigs and dug up sweet potatoes from the rebels' gardens. Since the sweet potato is the staff of life to the Kapauku, that was a significant loss.

After a month of this raiding, the battle began to turn in favor of the government. When the Dutch Navy brought in the Marines, some of the missionary women were flown out to Biak. A large group of Kapauku from one of the sister lakes joined the government and, from their position behind the Obano group, drove the enemy out of the hills into the hands of the Marines.

Although the fighting was over, the tension remained for a long time. In that culture, wars are considered won by the side inflicting the heaviest death toll. By that measure, the warriors from Obano still considered themselves the victors.

16

Overland to the Ilaga

With our one Cessna still under repair following the accident at Homeyo, and our newest one destroyed at Obano, The Christian and Missionary Alliance in New Guinea was temporarily without an aircraft. That meant that all our interior missionaries were faced with the curtailment of supplies.

Just as they had done after the loss of the Sealand, MAF's pilots rallied to assist us. They generously changed their flight schedules to accommodate our missionaries' needs in addition to the work they were already doing for other mission agencies on the island.

Even though MAF's help was considerable, they had only one aircraft at that time, and a very small one at that. I believed it was important to develop more and alternate capabilities for moving supplies.

So, with the permission of our field leaders, I contracted with Kroonduif, the local subsidiary of the Dutch airline KLM, to fly a Beaver aircraft for the government. Translated, Kroonduif is "Crown Dove," the name of a magnificent native New Guinea bird with fluffy light blue feathers and a massive crown of lacy plumes on its head. Under our agreement and in exchange for my work, the Mission would receive a commensurate amount of free flying hours as I flew for the government.

This was indeed an answer to prayer. Although it had only one engine, just like the Cessna, the DeHavilland Beaver was a much larger plane and had a more powerful engine. With one Beaver flight we could carry as much cargo as in two Cessna flights. By using Kroonduif's Beaver, we were able to keep the supply lines open to the Baliem and to the Wissel Lakes.

On my first Beaver flight to the interior, I was accompanied by Rev. Robert Chrisman, Area Secretary, and Rev. L.L. King who at that time was Foreign Secretary for the Alliance. He recalls the flight:

> I was in New Guinea for five days to brief Mr. Chrisman on the problems peculiar to this field. Don Gibbons and Gordon Larson were on a difficult overland trek from the Wissel Lakes to locate the Ilaga Valley and assess its potential for our Mission's occupation. A radio re-

port from the two men indicated that they had arrived in the Ilaga but needed medicine for one of them who was sick. Also, their battery was too weak for further transmissions. A battery charger was desperately needed.

With that, Ed removed one of the doors of the plane and loaded aboard a battery charger, the kind operated by pedaling a bicycle-type device. Then, with Mr. Chrisman in the copilot's seat and I in the back seat, we took off at daylight from Sentani. . . .

Upon arriving over the Ilaga Valley, Ed began to systematically crisscross the area in search of the two men. When at last we saw Gibbons and Larson, one of them was making wild gesticulations to get our attention while the other sat motionless, obviously too ill to exert himself. Soon we pushed overboard the battery charger rig and medicine, and resumed our journey toward the Wissel Lakes.

Sitting in the back seat of the airplane without its door was not easy. The continual blast of air made me bitterly cold. Now, added to this was the frightening realization that an impenetrable cloud cover had settled over the entire area with its 13,000-foot mountain peaks. Pilot Ulrich took us above the clouds and circled for what seemed an inordinately long time. Finally he located a crack in the clouds and headed for it. When at long last we saw the coastal waters below us, we took a direct course to Nabire, where, exceedingly low on fuel, we landed. I've always been thankful that Ed's skill and caution brought us safely through that experience.

On other flights, we used the large capacity of the Beaver to carry loads of lumber. With the number of missionaries on the increase in the Baliem, there was always a need for more building materials. At that point, highland supplies of timber had not yet been developed. In fact, early mission planners had seen references in the reports of the Archbold expedition that indicated a scarcity of lumber suitable for building, so they made their plans for aluminum houses and other structures accordingly.

There is considerable difference between the lumber we are familiar with in the States, smooth, dry and evenly cut, and the lumber in New Guinea, which is mostly rough cut, damp and varying in width, thickness and length.

On one flight, with a cabin full of such wood, I began to feel itching around my neck. I was at 8,000 feet, halfway to the Baliem. Soon I was engulfed by hundreds of fire ants. They had been aroused from their nests in the wood by the vibrations of the plane's engine, and perhaps also by the cooler temperatures of the higher altitude. By the time I reached the Baliem, I was covered with red blotches on my hands, arms, neck and face. My head felt as if it were on fire from the stings of those caught in my hair. It was a frightening experience.

During the almost six months of flying the Beaver, I was able not only to keep delivering supplies, but was also able to accumulate a sizable surplus. There was a savings of thousands of dollars to the Mission because all fuel was also paid for by Kroonduif for our flights.

After the arrival of our new Cessna, I stopped flying the Beaver. However, this contact with Kroonduif led to an exciting opportunity for me a few years later when MAF took over the Alliance flying program in 1957.

The warring that had erupted at Obano was hardly over when Ken and I decided to trek into the Ilaga. Now that it was obligatory for all airstrips to be inspected by a pilot before the first landing, the purpose of our trip was to do just that. We assembled our supplies, decided on which carriers to hire (not an easy job given the remaining tensions) and planned our route. Although the war was over, there was still considerable unrest around the Wissel Lakes. The killing of the Indonesian missionaries at Obano and the destruction of our plane made for a less-than-stable situation in that whole area.

The valley of the Ilaga River had been reached initially by Jerry and Ken in 1951. Later that year, Jerry, along with a Dutch government party, walked through the Ilaga to the upper Ibele Valley which overlooked the Baliem. They noted that some of the people in both the Ilaga and Ibele Valleys had the same clan names and therefore would be considered to be Dani. Gordon Larson, a linguist who was one of the first missionaries to live in the Ilaga, explains:

> The majority of the population in Ilaga was Dani (Western Dani as distinct from Grand Valley Dani, as we later learned). Don Gibbons and I were assigned to make a survey trip, not just to the main Ilaga Valley, but down-valley into unexplored territory in search of an area with more Uhunduni (as we then identified the Damal) where an airstrip might be made for the Sealand. That was June of 1954.
>
> We were raided, and returned home after twenty-eight days of trekking, deeply disappointed for what we perceived as failure. Tribal warfare soon after the raid broke out in the Ilaga, making it impossible for us to make a second trip until almost two years later in April of 1956.
>
> I remember how burdened Al Lewis, Dick Lenehan and Ed Ulrich were for the then unreached Damal tribespeople. I remember Al, fresh back from Canada, telling us how so many people were praying for the Damal and their conversion.
>
> On the second trip, we traveled with Ken Troutman. We had an Australian-

> made transceiver—a heavy one with a six-volt battery—to maintain contact with Enarotali and with Ed in the air. . . . We began clearing the flat area at Milivak, where the Beoga airstrip is now located, and radioed for Ed to fly over the area to see if it might be made into an airfield. He flew over it while we talked with him on our radio. I recall him saying that with the cloud buildup along the steep slopes, it was like looking down inside of an empty ice cream cone. He said that the site would not be workable for an airstrip.

It would be several more years before the Beoga airstrip would be built and finally opened by MAF pilot, George Boggs. Because of the vertiginous turns required on the approach, George referred to it as "Vomit Valley." But, back to the opening of the Ilaga, Gordon continues:

> On our third trip, Don and I had difficulty getting either Moni or Ekari carriers since open hostilities still existed between the Ilaga and the other valleys to the north and east. So . . . Don separated from our party to search for carriers, and I was alone . . . for a full month. Ed tried to drop supplies to me, but cloud coverage prevented it. My hand-cranked generator would not give enough power to broadcast on the radio, only enough to

> hear, but only faintly. It was a discouraging time. But the Lord assured us we would reach the Ilaga. Don finally located Kapauku carriers, we made it over the high plateau to Ilaga by September of 1956 and began working on the airstrip.

Now, with Gordon and Don already in the valley, Ken and I began our trek. Most of the first day we traveled by native boats up small rivers, then smaller streams. These waterways took us to our first foothills, and then the real trekking began.

From the very first day, we became concerned by the taunts of local people as we passed by, a carryover from the Obano war. Whether it was actually a precursor of possible violence or not, it certainly was a threat to our peace of mind and our desire to continue on—exactly the effect the Obano people intended, no doubt.

Among our supplies, we carried a battery and radio. When we made contact with Enarotali, we learned of more threats, but we did not inform our carriers. We were certain they would refuse to continue if they knew there was possible trouble ahead.

On the third day, wet and muddy, we arrived at Homeyo, the Cutts' station. During the next few days, we repacked our supplies, assigned various loads to our carriers, then set off for the Ilaga. This was humid tropical rain forest country where, for the next thirteen days, we averaged only four miles a day.

The first stream was about fifteen feet wide and very swift-flowing. Only a single log offered passage across the rushing water. Sure that our trek was about to end right there, I finally, out of desperation, got down on my hands and knees and slithered across. To have slipped off would have been fatal.

Further into the rain forest, the whole atmosphere became depressing. We were constantly wet. The jungle foliage blocked out any sun. We seemed to be in perpetual twilight. Although we had shoes with metal cleats in the soles and heels, most of our walking—struggling—was not on paths but over wet tree roots. Even with cleated shoes, our footing was very poor. I can't even guess at how many times we slipped and fell.

Late each afternoon, we set up camp for the night. Ken and I put up our tents, and the carriers cut poles and large leaves with which to make their own tents. We carried dehydrated vegetables, including cabbage, carrots and potatoes, our only food during the trek. We boiled water, both for drinking and for cooking the vegetables.

At one point, while trying to traverse a steep mountain slope covered by those slippery roots, I felt a sharp pain in my side. At that point in our trip, I was probably as far away from any outside help as one could be. After we rested for a short time, the pain was gone, and we continued higher and higher into the mountain range.

Because of the dampness and altitude, it became bitterly cold at night. Our carriers in their native dress—actually undress—shivered from head to toe. And the closer we got to the Ilaga, the more restless they became. They knew about the unfriendly people in this area. Only with great persuasion were we able to convince them to continue.

During one of our night stops, we came in contact with a small group. They seemed friendly enough and offered to let us camp in their area for the night. Ken thought it might be prudent if he and I shared the same two-man tent. It might keep us alert—and safe.

After a hard day's struggle on the trail, sleep comes easily, even when one tries to keep one ear open for possible danger. But this night, there was a great need to be cautious.

Not long after we lay down on our mats, we heard movement outside. The "friendly" men were surrounding our tent and sticking their long spears into the ground all around it. We were literally in a cage. The one good thing about that was that it was better than if they had stuck the spears through the tent and into us!

"What are you carrying?" they asked Ken, who knew their language. Apparently they were suspicious because somehow they had learned we had several steel ax heads with us. The native axes had blades made of sharpened stone; steel axes were a highly prized commodity.

We did not want to admit to having ax heads. We knew if they did find a supply that we would probably be killed. Instead, we offered the head of the group one of the steel axes, all the time trying to convey to him that we had only two, and the other one was for a chief at our destination. It was a psychologically prudent move since, by giving an ax head to the headman, he would be elevated in the eyes of his followers. It seemed to pacify them.

Eager to get on our way the next morning, we skipped breakfast and headed down a trail. However, we soon became aware that the men were furtively shadowing us. We decided to ignore them and struggled on. Where would we find a suitable campsite tonight? Or would we? That was the burning question of the day.

During the entire trek, we tried to make our camp on high ground. Not only was the view good, but we could often see the mountain where we'd slept the previous night, and we could make radio contact with our base and keep track of the flight schedule of our Cessna being flown by Bill Paul.

One day, we heard the plane fly overhead, but because of the jungle canopy were unable to see him. It was a bit discouraging when we estimated that the airplane was covering in three minutes what we were taking three days to cover!

Each day climbing higher, we finally reached a plateau at 14,000 feet above sea level. Off to our right were the snowcapped peaks of the Carstensz Range. Walking was extremely difficult. The plateau was a marshy bog with clumps of grass spreading throughout the whole area. To avoid sinking ankle-deep into the icy bog, we tried jumping from grass clump to grass clump. But at 14,000 feet and carrying a backpack, jumping from clump to clump soon caused shortness of breath and headaches.

Crossing this plateau also were swift roaring streams supplied by melting snow and daily rains. Although these streams were only about three feet wide, they had steep grassy banks. If one missed on the jump, he would land in the chilling water. One carrier jumped and did not quite reach the opposite bank. Unfortunately, he was carrying our radio. It was completely filled with water and proved unusable for the remainder of the trip.

Our first concern when that happened was for our wives: What would they think when they didn't hear from us? It was frustrating that we couldn't communicate with them and dispel the apprehension we knew would quickly invade their hearts and minds. They knew how untractable was the jungle, how capricious the winds, how unpredictable the response of native peoples. They were still all too mindful of the freshness and pain of Al's loss. And, as always, there was fear of the unknown.

As we slowly made our way across the plateau, cold rain, sleet and wind kept us wet from head to toe. Finding a suitable place to set up our tents was difficult enough for Ken and me. But the carriers fared much worse. With no trees or bushes to protect them from the weather, they simply huddled under a tarp.

Although it was dry inside our small tents, we still had a problem. With the tent closed to keep out the elements, we soon used up all the oxygen inside and had to zip open the flap and stick out our heads in order to catch our breath. Even under the best conditions, it was hard to breathe at 14,000 feet.

After the trials and discomforts of the rain forest and then the plateau, it was a great thrill to descend into the Ilaga Valley to meet Gordon and Don. Janet Steiger, wife of an MAF pilot, wrote in *Wings over Shangri-La:* "Ulrich undoubtedly gets first prize for the longest, most grueling trek made by our pilots. It took twenty days and, for a man not accustomed to trails, it was tough."

Larson and Gibbons had built a small building for themselves while the work of constructing the airstrip was going on. Ken and I were welcomed with a meal of taro root. Raw, it is poisonous; fried, it tastes like heavy bread. We found the men somewhat discouraged. It was easy to get that way in such an isolated and unyielding environment.

At times, building the Ilaga strip had involved up to 1,000 Dani and Damal removing up to three feet of peat and mud in some areas or clearing a knoll in others. Sometimes, however, when they felt threatened by what could possibly be an enemy attack, the workers would grab their weapons and run off to defend themselves.

Gordon and Don also knew about the uprising at Obano during which their load of supplies on the Cessna had been demolished and several people killed. And they knew of threats which had been made against the government and missionaries at Enarotali—including their families. Then, during a drop of supplies in late November or early December 1956, came the discouraging report from MAF pilot Dave Steiger that the airstrip was so soft and wet that it would never be landable. Now, however, less rain and more sunshine had hardened the strip. I believed it would be usable—eventually.

After a week of intense effort to complete the work, we outlined the edges with black ashes and marked off a center line. We radioed Sentani and asked Bill Paul to drop a load of supplies on the strip and to make several prelanding patterns to assess the best approach route.

Bill arrived the following day. We expected that he would circle several times, then drop the items. Instead, to our surprise, he landed!

Following our Homeyo accident, the Department of Civil Aviation had given strict orders that all future Alliance airstrips were to be physically inspected by me, as chief pilot, to be followed by a complete written report of the strip. Upon receiving that report, Mr. Hamers, the Director of Civil Aviation would accompany me on the first landing. At that time, if all went well, permission could be given to officially open the airstrip.

Some time later, after the fact, Bill brought Mr. Hamers in to inspect the strip. After a morning of pacing off the length, checking drainage patterns, marking soft spots and recommending improvements, Mr. Hamers gave conditional approval so that the Larson and Gibbons families could be flown in.

The Dani people at Ilaga soon became used to the sight of airplanes. They, along with those in many other areas of New Guinea, were learning that our airplanes, far from causing sickness and death, as they once believed, often became the means for bringing life and healing, both physical and spiritual. Within a year of the opening of the strip, thousands of Ilaga, Damal and Dani turned from being vicious warriors to becoming enthusiastic disciples of Jesus Christ. And, within the next few years, thousands more would follow.

17

Air America

In 1957, the Mission's Board of Managers reassessed their aviation program in New Guinea. A number of factors were considered, including the high costs of maintaining airplanes and personnel for a full-fledged program. The accidents, the loss of Al Lewis and the destruction of the airplane at Obano were also considered. More important to the decision, though, were the increasing presence and ministry of MAF in the area and their willingness to cooperate with the Alliance as well as other missions.

In some ways, that cooperation had begun with the close relationship we felt with MAF upon their arrival in New Guinea in 1954, about a year after the Alliance program in New Guinea had officially begun. Even in the first years, we shared tools, parts, supplies and sometimes even storage space. When they decided to use floats on their Piper Pacer, operating it from nearby Sentani Lake, we had served as check-outs to help their pilots practice water landings and takeoffs. Also, we assisted MAF in planning a seaplane ramp at the end of the road between our hangars and the lake.

Finally a decision was made. In April 1957, the Alliance transferred its airplanes, hangar and shop equipment to MAF for the payment of $1, thus terminating the nineteen years of the Alliance's pioneering aviation. Although individual missionaries in a few countries had owned and flown airplanes (the first recorded airplane use by a missionary was in 1924, in the Dominican Republic), The Christian and Missionary Alliance had become the first Mission to own aircraft when it purchased a Beechcraft on floats for the work in Borneo in 1938. (That aircraft was destroyed during the war to prevent its use by the advancing Japanese.)

Then, after the war, Al Lewis went to Borneo with a second Beechcraft, which was replaced by the first Sealand. That plane was used there until its destruction in 1951 while being flown to Java for repairs from a previous accident.

While Al Lewis was on a brief furlough, a pilot on loan from another Mission, had a takeoff accident in the Sealand. When Al returned to Borneo, he arranged for temporary repairs so that he could fly the plane to a depot for more permanent work. En route, as he was circling to land at a small island, rebels shot at the plane, rupturing a fuel tank. Al made an emergency landing in the rough sea, damaging the repair done earlier on the hull. He managed to beach the plane, but when he went to seek aid, sea water flooded into the cockpit, and corrosion damaged the aluminum craft beyond repair.

Years later, in 1969, the aviation program in Borneo, by then called Kalimantan, would be restarted by Missionary Aviation Fellowship, and even now continues, supporting a large Alliance work among the Dyak people.

It became clear that MAF would give wholehearted commitment to the support of our missionaries in New Guinea and that they would be as fully dedicated to that task as our own personnel had been. Within a few months, the Lenehans and the Pauls left for the United States and their subsequent ministries there. In farewell to all the airline support staff, the New Guinea Alliance missionary team sent us a warm letter of appreciation thanking us for our work among them. In part, it read:

> We wish to convey to you a small portion of our great appreciation for the work you have done in the opening up of this part of the Lord's vineyard. We who have been here pioneering in the tremendous task of opening the vast expanse of interior New Guinea to the preaching of the gospel of Christ can never forget the part you have played working side by side with us, bringing in our supplies by drop when there were no strips, coming in over

> the difficult trails to look for strip sites, coming in again to inspect the partially completed strips, doing the dangerous work of setting down planes on these strips for the initial landings, and then servicing our stations by bringing in load after load of all kinds of supplies on those imperfect, incomplete strips.
>
> We appreciate the courage you have displayed on our behalf as unto the Lord, flying day after day over vast stretches of uninhabited, awful terrain, dodging dangerous storms and cloud buildups in order to transport the supplies vital to our work.
>
> It is our prayer that as each of you prepare to enter other work, the Lord may guide and direct you and keep you in the center of His will. We pray that He may use you for His glory and that His richest blessings may attend your lives.

I was hired by Kroonduif, the KLM subsidiary airline for whom I had flown the Beaver earlier. Part of my duties was to help establish airline routes throughout Dutch New Guinea. Because of my background and experience, I had knowledge of the areas in which Kroonduif wished to establish those services. During this phase of flying I also flew established air routes, most of them with the Douglas DC-3, a venerable transport airplane known during the war as the C-47, "Gooney Bird" and "Dakota."

Newer, pioneer routes that were being developed were, appropriately, flown in an airplane called the Twin Pioneer, a short-field takeoff and landing (STOL) aircraft. The Twin Pioneer had been developed for flying in and out of short airstrips and had been used extensively in British military work in the jungles of Malaya (now known as Malaysia). It has a wing span of seventy-seven feet, three large tails for good control at low speeds and a large cabin for sixteen passengers and baggage. It was the ideal choice for the small unimproved airstrips in New Guinea.

Kroonduif also expanded their fleet of Beavers, ultimately using three on their “pioneer services” to interior mountain strips. Some of these airstrips were specially built by the government, but several were Mission airstrips into which I had flown previously. A Beaver converted to floats was used at the Wissel Lakes.

In 1956, the government began developing a large base at Wamena in the Baliem Valley, about five miles from the river landing site we had used for the Sealand, and they moved their post to a place right beside the new airstrip. One of my assignments with Kroonduif was to evaluate the potential for this airstrip. Today, the runway at Wamena is over a mile long, is paved and accommodates large aircraft including Indonesian military C-130 Hercules and occasional twin-engine jets.

After several years with Kroonduif, living at their base at Biak, we returned to the United

States, and from 1959 to 1962 lived again in Western Pennsylvania. I was pilot for a construction firm and the manager of the Sharon, Pennsylvania airport where I began a flying club, a flight instruction school and a charter service.

An unexpected and joyous "chance" meeting took place one time when I was flying back from the Bahamas after a charter trip there: I ran into Dr. L.L. King in Raleigh, North Carolina. Actually, it wasn't a serendipity at all—it was God who brought us together on that occasion:

> Ed and I had many opportunities for fellowship in many parts of the world, but one meeting here in the States was a very real answer to prayer. I had just concluded my meetings at a church in the southeast. Friends delivered me to the airport for my flight back to New York. We saw no need for them to wait until I had boarded, so they dropped me off and left.
>
> As I entered the terminal, I had a strange feeling. There were no people! Many of the shops were darkened. It was late, but I was on time for my flight.
>
> When the check-in counter was also darkened, I became quite uneasy. Then I noticed the sign: "All Flights Canceled Due to Weather." I found myself alone and wondered what to do. I had no transportation, no motel room, and, after

> checking through my briefcase, no phone number of my recent host!
>
> I began to pray. It seemed like I had just committed my situation to the Lord when Ed Ulrich walked into that darkened terminal waiting area. I could see the shock on his face when he recognized me sitting there alone with my baggage at my side.
>
> Ed had come to check the weather. . . . He had landed earlier to refuel, and then the airport had closed. . . .
>
> Soon I told him about my problem. Ed said that he had a rented car and a motel room with two double beds. . . . He persuaded me to join him for the night, then check out the situation in the morning. What an answer to prayer!

In 1961, I was recruited for an airline job in Southeast Asia. Within a week of applying, I reported to Washington D.C. for an interview. There I learned that the airline was Air America, a covert operation of the Central Intelligence Agency with operations in Laos, Thailand and Vietnam. At one time or another I would be based in each of those countries. I was accepted for employment, based largely, I think, on the recent experience I'd had on DC-3 aircraft in New Guinea. In the early '60s, not many pilots had air time on such old airplanes and, of course, they were the most plentiful types in that part of the world.

Following my interview with the CIA official, I was sent to Taipei, Taiwan, for further evaluation and was interviewed there by the chief pilot and the vice president of the "company." At that time, Taipei was the overseas headquarters for Air America and also for CAT (Civil Air Transport), another covert operation. CAT operated commercially as Mandarin Jet, with cabin decor modeled on the traditional Chinese motif.

I made a point, during my interview, to give my testimony, to describe my New Guinea experiences and also to express my interest in working with the Alliance missionaries serving in Southeast Asia. I emphasized that I was not interested in the "soldier of fortune" aspect that attracted so many others to this kind of work. The chief pilot was very receptive and gave me permission to assist the Mission program as long as it did not add to the direct cost of the overall operation of Air America.

How all that would work out in practical terms remained to be seen. In fact, it turned out to be much more rewarding than I could have anticipated.

18

Metal Wings, Invisible Wings

Shortly after we arrived in Vientiane, Laos with Air America, I was appointed chief pilot and deputy base manager. My mission orientation was still a top priority. Thanks to earlier agreements I had made with my superiors in Air America, I would be able to assist the Alliance Mission and missionaries by scheduling supplies, personnel and vehicles on flights that were not fully loaded with "customer" freight or passengers. "Customer" was in-house jargon referring to the military and political missions that were the bulk of our business.

In many cases, our up-country landing strips were near mission stations, a convenient arrangement, indeed. I was able to continue these services until we returned to the U.S. fourteen years later.

During those years, I had more than enough excitement to last a lifetime. Such covert military operations were an extremely dangerous business. The statistics speak for themselves: more than eighty Air America pilots and over 200 crew members died during those years. Some were shot down. Many crashed in bad weather. These were not inexperienced people. Most were veteran flyers. Their average age was forty. Aviation writers described them as some of the most experienced pilots in the world.

I turned fifty while serving in Laos and remember that birthday well. On this occasion, I was flying a C-123 cargo plane. The weather could only be described as "horrible." We were distributing bags of rice and drums of fuel to other interior airstrips. Our first stop was on a high plateau in northwestern Thailand where the borders of Burma, Laos and Thailand meet. This is the notorious "Golden Triangle," a hotbed of criminal activity and drug trafficking.

As we were preparing to take off, the weather deteriorated rapidly. Heavy thunderclouds with heavy rain seemed to engulf us. It seemed that we were actually within the storm itself. There was a distinct possibility that we could be trapped here on this high plateau for the night or longer. Just as in New Guinea, there were no reliable weather forecasts. But after several hours of waiting out the storms, my crew and I spotted the beginnings of small breaks in the weather. Finally we took off and worked our way around the clouds and eventually landed safely at our lowland base.

The film *Air America,* released in 1990, was a gross misrepresentation of even the simplest facts about Air America and our part in the air war in Southeast Asia. Besides the fact that none of us looked like Mel Gibson, it was a flippant account of what we stood for and what we carried out. In fact, I and a number of former Air America pilots tried very hard to get the producers to be more realistic instead of depicting Air America pilots as gunrunners, drug-runners and womanizing cowboys all trying to get rich off the war. The serious issues of why we were there and the gravity of our missions were glossed over in that movie. The lives and deaths of brave men were caricaturized and distorted for cheap laughs.

Unlike those in the movie, our planes were not armed, nor were they combat ready. However, I did wear a flak jacket and carried an Israeli-made Uzi submachine gun for protection. On several occasions, my plane was damaged by gunfire. One time, our radio, which was mounted in the instrument panel, was shot out. Officially, we flew "rice" (food) and "hard rice" (ammunition), transported personnel between bases, relocated refugees and rescued combat pilots who had gone down behind enemy lines.

One early series of missions I flew was an infrared study of heavy artillery. Thai soldiers on the ground below us would, at a prearranged time, fire large guns. We would then fly over the gun emplacements, sometimes only 200 feet above them, in a C-47 equipped with infrared cameras designed to register the heat from objects on film. Our crew on these flights included ten scientists, among them the world's expert in infrared photography and analysis. As the heat from the guns dissipated, the infrared images of the most recently fired ones differed from ones fired earlier.

Through that experiment, military analysts in Vietnam could determine how recently a particular enemy weapon had fired, and could usually pinpoint the particular gun emplacement from which the shells had been fired. Military aircraft were then sent on bombing runs to remove the threat. Those test flights, obviously extremely risky, were made in mountain areas, at night, at minimum altitudes.

Amazingly, the infrared equipment was sensitive enough to pick up images of elephants the Vietcong sometimes used to carry supplies. We could even identify sick elephants—one with a fever would appear as a brighter image than the elephants who were well. Our equipment was an important way to track troop movement.

When Lon Nol became prime minister of Cambodia, edging the country away from communism, I was ordered to lead a covert series of flights into Cambodia to bolster his new government. Before dawn, three C-123s took off from Paksay, Laos, heading for Phnom Penh. The men on board were carrying instructions to Lon Nol's administration. While they briefed the government officials, those of us in the crew were told to "lie low" during the day and then return to Laos when night fell.

One afternoon in Phnom Penh, I had my picture taken standing next to a Russian-made MiG-17. A whole fleet of MiGs, with the Cambodian insignia on them, was parked and loaded with American bombs. I was intrigued by the clever way in which the bomb attachment mechanisms had been "jury-rigged," that is, improvised so that a Russian-made aircraft could carry American bombs.

Under the new prime minister, Lon Nol, Cambodia was on the defensive against the Khmer Rouge. Russian-made MiG fighters once used against Cambodia were now in the hands of the new anti-communist government. In order to use them, the Air Force painted Cambodian insignia on their wings and tails. Now that the Americans were supplying the bombs, special modifications had to be made so that the new bombs could fit on the racks originally designed only to fit Russian munitions.

Another operation I was responsible for earned headlines around the world—the evacuation of thousands of Hmong mountain people from the Plain of Jars to safer locations. There was no airstrip there, so we selected an aircraft, the Lockheed C-130 Hercules, that could operate from unimproved surfaces. Our "unimproved surface" was a huge grassy field.

On each flight we loaded from 400 to 600 persons on board—standing room only—holding onto cargo straps we had secured from one wall to the other every ten feet. Needless to say, there was no in-flight beverage service or any other amenity, but for many of the 25,000 people we airlifted between January and April 1970, this free ride on Air America saved their lives.

When our Alliance station at Sam Thong, Laos was overrun by the enemy, the home of missionaries Wayne and Minnie Persons was destroyed. After loyalist soldiers had recaptured the village and airstrip, I was assigned to make a survey of the damage. The pilot dropped me off, but to my consternation didn't stay on the ground while I took the pictures. Instead, once he dropped me off, he took off and circled high overhead, apparently unwilling to lose an aircraft if someone ambushed me.

One of our carefully guarded secrets in Thailand was the air base at Takli. During the Vietnam War, this base was considered a military secret and was strictly off-limits for anyone not authorized to fly there. Some of our Air America pilots operated from Takli on what were called "black flight" (secret) missions. Airplanes in use for such operations were "cleaned," that is, all items were removed that could identify who owned and operated the airplane. Even the tail number was assigned to a similar plane operating within Southeast Asia, so that if the plane flying the secret mission was shot down, the CIA would have what was called "deniability," and could say, "That is not one of ours. Look, we have that tail number flying here in Laos."

All Air America pilots had been briefed on "company" policy: If we were shot down, the CIA would deny that we were ever connected with them. In other words, we weren't to expect any massive search and rescue operation if we had a problem!

A U-2 reconnaissance plane operated from Takli as well. This was kept as a very strict secret. One of the pilots under my command was a U-2 pilot who frequently flew missions over mainland China. In a little-known operation in the '70s, night air drops into areas of China still loyal to Chiang Kai-Shek were made during famines and the Cultural Revolution using a Boeing 727. This jet operated out of Takli and was equipped with special floor tracks which helped the cargo move swiftly to the drop bay in the rear of the aircraft.

Takli was also the base used for the F-111 low altitude flights the Air Force made during the war years. When we were flying missions out of Takli, we were not permitted to make any outside contacts. One amenity was that meals were served on a twenty-four-hour basis to accommodate the irregular schedules.

Our years in Southeast Asia were not entirely devoted to the spy trade, however. While we lived in Vientiane, Laos, I was treasurer and board member of the Alliance-sponsored International Church there. The positions I held with Air America also became useful to the in-country Alliance missionary program. Because I knew the flying schedule, I was able to work with Malcolm Sawyer, the field business manager, to help supply interior stations. I often notified Mac about upcoming flights to various stations, and he would prepare a load of supplies or notify personnel who needed to go there or arrange the transportation of a vehicle (since most of our aircraft were designed to carry vehicles at least the size of a jeep or a small truck). Of course, any supplies being carried were on a "space available" basis.

Over fourteen years, the monetary savings to the Mission were substantial. Malcolm and Helen Sawyer recall our years in Vientiane:

> The Ulrichs were always a part of the missionary team, attending weekly staff prayer meetings and sharing the burdens and concerns for the work among the Lao, Khamoo and Meo (Hmong) people. God used them on many occasions to provide a special need among the missionaries. . . .
>
> The months when Elaine was in the States with their daughters in school, Ed lived at the Mission guest house in one of the rooms in the back always referred to as "moldy manor." There was no air-conditioning—only a clunky old fan which did little to alleviate the heat and humidity. We were always grateful when Ed paid his board with treats from the American commissary.
>
> On one occasion he brought a canned

> ham from the U.S., a rare item in far-off Laos. That very day, one of the Lao teachers at our Bible Training Center came to show us a tiny baby girl he had purchased at the morning market. We calculated that the mother had sold the child for the same price Ed had paid for the ham! We were grateful that the child now had a Christian family to care for it.

When we were transferred to Bangkok, Thailand, our family, along with several others, began to meet for Sunday worship in a renovated garage at the Alliance Guest House. Interest and attendance grew, and, under the leadership of missionary Bill Carlson, we moved to an auditorium in one of Bangkok's leading hotels. Our presence in this central facility enabled us to reach many more people, including American military and government personnel. Further expansion eventually led to the building of the Bangkok Evangelical Church, an attractive structure just off Sukhumvit Boulevard, one of Bangkok's main streets.

By then, the scope of the ministry had expanded far beyond the humble beginnings as a Bible study, and we hired a full-time pastor, Rev. William Nabors. He recalls:

> One of the couples attending the group was Ed and Elaine Ulrich along with their three daughters, Lynne, Laurie and Leslie. They became staunch sup-

> porters of the group and were used of God to see it established as a church.
>
> During our first year in Bangkok, the group was organized as the Evangelical Church of Bangkok. Ed was elected to serve on the Governing Board of the church and also served as Sunday school superintendent. Elaine was the church pianist and taught the adult Sunday school class.

While I was stationed in Bangkok, my office was at Bangkok's international airport, the same airport where Al Lewis and I had been detained by red tape in 1953. During the Tet offensive in Vietnam, a number of Alliance stations were threatened, and some were overrun. Several of our missionaries were captured by the Vietcong, and some were killed. (See *To Vietnam with Love* by Charles E. Long, #12 in The Jaffray Collection of Missionary Portraits.)

During this terrible time, two men visited my office: Dr. Nathan Bailey, who was president of The Christian and Missionary Alliance, and Rev. Grady Mangham, the field representative for Vietnam. They needed to get into Vietnam to review the situation. Could I help them get there?

I called the American ambassador to Thailand and explained how imperative it was that these men get to Saigon. Ambassador Unger suggested I call the Thai Minister of Aviation. In a matter of minutes, he had authorized a special Air America flight from Bangkok to Saigon. I made the arrangements with our Saigon station, notified the standby air crew in Bangkok, telephoned the hangar crew to prepare the plane and called the airport tower for special clearance. Within two hours, Dr. Bailey and Rev. Mangham were in the air, bound for Saigon— the only passengers on a special Air America flight.

While living in Southeast Asia, our daughters attended Dalat School. However, when I was transferred to Saigon, Elaine and the girls moved back to Pennsylvania so that the girls could continue schooling, including college. I moved into the Alliance Guest House.

Perhaps what I cherish most from the years in Laos, Thailand and Vietnam is the number of missionaries who became my close friends. Such a loving and dedicated group of people would be hard to find anywhere.

Despite the moves and separations, we thank God that our family has thrived over the years.

Ted, a retired U.S. Army major, is married to Judy. They live in Virginia where he is a senior engineering analyst for Newport News Shipbuilding. Judy is a special education administrator for the city of Portsmouth, Virginia. Ted has a son, Kevin, and a daughter, Deborah (Walbrecher).

Lynne is married to John Evans, son of Alliance missionaries to India. They have made a career of teaching in American/International schools. So far, this has taken them to India, Pakistan, Jordan, Zaire, Hong Kong and Morocco. They have two children, both teachers. Jeremy lives in Greensboro, North Carolina, and Rachel lives in Phoenix, Arizona.

Laurie lives in Arlington, Virginia, and is an executive secretary in an international law firm.

Leslie is married to Patrick McBane, an associate pastor at Fifth Avenue Community Church (Foursquare) in Youngstown, Ohio. She is a kindergarten teacher and reading specialist. They have two daughters, Emily and Allison.

As Elaine and I reflect upon our family and the years God has given us to serve Him together, surely the pioneering days in New Guinea and the stressful years in Southeast Asia were not always easy. But through it all, God has proved Himself faithful as we joined the team and became a part of what He was doing. Myron Bromley describes it as follows:

> There are places in the world where the work of missions would have been slower and harder without airplanes. In the Baliem Valley, it would have been impossible. On the metal wings of airplanes and on the invisible wings of prayer, we who have served there have been carried